THE
BREAD
BAKER'S
MANUAL

THE CREATIVE COOKING SERIES
Every recipe in each of our cookbooks has been
kitchen tested by the authors.

ROSALIE CHENEY FISKE and JOANNE KOCH POTEE
are both knowledgcable bread bakers, based in Petersham,
Massachusetts, with many years of experience between them.
They also give bread-baking demonstrations.

THE BREAD BAKER'S MANUAL

The How's and Why's of Creative Bread Making

ROSALIE CHENEY FISKE

JOANNE KOCH POTEE

Illustrations by Barbara Sleigh Ellis

A SPECTRUM BOOK

PRENTICE-HALL, INC., *Englewood Cliffs, N.J. 07632*

Library of Congress Cataloging in Publication Data

FISKE, ROSALIE CHENEY.
    The bread baker's manual.

    (The Creative cooking series) (A Spectrum Book)
    Includes index.
    1. Bread.   I. Potee, Joanne Koch (date)
joint author.   II. Title.   III. Series.
TX769.F56   641.8'15   77-17856
ISBN 0-13-081638-8
ISBN 0-13-081620-5 (pbk.)

© 1978 by Prentice-Hall, Inc.,
Englewood Cliffs, New Jersey 07632

A SPECTRUM BOOK

Printed in the United States of America

PRENTICE-HALL INTERNATIONAL, INC., *London*

PRENTICE-HALL OF AUSTRALIA PTY. LIMITED, *Sydney*

PRENTICE-HALL OF CANADA, LTD., *Toronto*

PRENTICE-HALL OF INDIA PRIVATE LIMITED, *New Delhi*

PRENTICE-HALL OF JAPAN, INC., *Tokyo*

PRENTICE-HALL OF SOUTHEAST ASIA PTE. LTD., *Singapore*

WHITEHALL BOOKS LIMITED, *Wellington, New Zealand*

To our husbands,
who manfully ate their way
through a veritable mountain
of experimental loaves.

Contents

3 Flours and Cereals 43

Mixing Methods   55

 What Went Wrong?   61

RECIPES

 6 Kneaded Yeast Breads 67

7 Unkneaded or Batter Breads 101

8 Festive Yeast Breads 115

Sourdough Breads 133

Preface

Bread making is easy. And fun!

With the ever-increasing numbers of bread books being written by the most expert cooks, one more addition to the bookshelves must be enough to make the prospective bread baker shake her—or his—head in bewilderment.

The importance of this book, and what makes it different from those others on the shelves, lies in its showing both beginners and experienced bakers how to create their own recipes. Only by truly making one's own breads from recipe to fragrant, golden loaf, can one know the real joy and satisfaction of baking. The many excellent recipes given here are a bonus.

We have set forth basic methods, simply and clearly. There is a section on natural grains and other ingredients, including spices and herbs, describing their properties and telling how they can be combined to give the best textured and flavored loaf. Other, less common ingredients are described, including cereals, leftovers, vegetables, fruits, and stocks. You will learn how to maintain a proper balance between the liquid and solid ingredients. You will find the basic recipes for yeast, batter, quick breads, and sourdough breads a most useful framework for your own creations. More than ever today we are all interested in getting the most for our money as well as maximum nutritional value by using the best natural ingredients.

For those whose bread-baking efforts in the past have been less than successful, there is a chapter called "What Went Wrong?" This section is based on the innumerable questions put to us by many bread makers who have had problems in achieving the perfect loaf.

Practice first with the recipes in this book, then try your own. Be imaginative. If you follow the basic principles described here, you will soon be creating your own excellent loaves. Have fun, and good baking!

We are grateful to our friends for their help, encouragement, and prodding, and especially to our testers, Helen L. Coolidge, Barbara A. Corey, and Patricia R. Pratt. Our special thanks to Lucy G. Raup for starting us on the sourdough path, for advising us on the sourdough chapter, and for testing many of the recipes in this book; and to Gale Potee, for his painstaking proofreading.

THE HISTORY OF BREAD

1 Ten Thousand Years in a Minute

As you munch on a slice of bread, have you ever given a thought to its beginnings? Its lineage is older than the history it has so greatly influenced.

When early nomadic man learned that bread could be made of crushed acorns or beechnuts and water, and cooked in the sun, he forsook his nomadic ways. No longer was he dependent on wild game and forced to follow its migrations; he could live in one place. The next step was the discovery that wild grain made wholesome food. He harvested it, pounded it into meal with a stone, and baked the flat cakes in the ashes of his fire. An agrarian society was born, laying the foundations for today's urbanized living.

Wheat and barley were the earliest grains used, later followed by rye, buckwheat, Indian corn, beans, peas, potatoes, and rice. The earliest known bread was that found by archaeologists in the kitchen middens of the Swiss Lake Dwellers, baked ten thousand years ago.

The earliest records of stone milling of flour date back to 4000 B.C., when hand stones or querns were used. By 2000 B.C. many mills

3

were powered by slaves or cattle. The Greeks had introduced single waterwheel stones by 450 B.C. The Romans invented geared waterwheels with several stones and later windmills to grind their grain into flour. They also improved upon the Egyptian ovens.

Bread as we know it today was probably first baked in Egypt about five thousand years ago, where it became a fine art. The Egyptians raised wheat and barley; their tomb paintings at Thebes show them growing and harvesting wheat, grinding grain and dates with enormous stones, mixing the flour into a batter which they poured into long, narrow molds and baked in beehive-shaped ovens. They also made bread from the heart of a lotus plant.

These breads became the forerunners of our raised yeast breads. As the story goes, a baker mixed a batch of batter and forgot it. When he discovered it the next day, it had more than "doubled in bulk." Waste was not tolerated by the Pharoah and the baker was badly frightened, which was understandable, since the usual form of dismissal was the loss of one's head. He dared throw away only half the batter, mixing a new lot with the old. It is easy to imagine his fear when it rose again. He baked it anyway and found it good, and presented it to the Pharoah as his own creation. We can only hope he was made the first baker of the land.

The Egyptians used many exotic and fanciful molds to shape their breads, and bakery became an art. It became so highly regarded, in fact, that bread ovens were built in the temples and bakers equaled priests in importance.

Bread was baked in ancient Persia, and the Chinese discovered how to make a light bread from fermented dough about the same time as the Egyptians. Both Greece and Rome had many kinds of bread, using wheat, barley, rye, and rice. In Greece bread became part of the religious observance.

By 100 B.C. there were 258 commercial bakeries in Rome, producing loaves from wheat, barley, rye, and other grains, and even loaves of a beautiful whiteness. In 100 A.D. Emperor Trajan founded a school for bakers. Bakers' guilds were formed. Round loaves of bread stamped with the baker's name or device have been found in Pompeii. As time went on the bakers became highly regarded and respected, and some held public office.

In the Middle Ages, the oldest of the town guilds in Europe were the bakers' guilds. There were laws which protected bakers from unfair competition and the people from dishonest bakers. Each guild had its own seal which it stamped on its loaves, and a few of these loaves are found in museums today.

Not until the last two centuries could any but the nobly born have white bread. During the reign of William and Mary all wheat flour was taken to the cities, and the peasants were left with rye and barley bread and oatcakes. Today every nation has its own favorite and distinctive breads. American bread is unlike that found in Europe, in that it has milk, sweetening, and shortening in addition to the flour, water, salt, and leavening found in European breads.

BASICS

2 Tips, Terms, and Ingredients

BAKING

Preheat your oven to the desired temperature for at least 15 minutes before putting loaves in to bake. The oven has reached the desired temperature when the oven light goes off the second time. There will be less fluctuation in temperature if you don't skimp on preheating.

Bake on the middle shelf, with pans two inches from each other and from the sides of the oven. Place them on the diagonal for better heat circulation. Do not crowd your oven. Unless the oven is very large, two big pans or four small ones are sufficient at one time.

Do not open the oven door for the first 10 minutes. It is during this critical period that the final rising takes place.

When the bread is done (see "Doneness"), remove regular yeast breads from the pans immediately and cool them on their sides on wire racks. For easier removal sweet yeast and quick breads should cool in the pans for 10 to 15 minutes after being taken from the oven, until they are strong enough to stand up alone.

Longer baking gives a thicker crust than shorter baking. (See "Ovens" and "Temperatures.") For baking French bread, see "Ovens."

9

BAKING POWDER

All quick bread recipes in this book call for double-acting baking powder. A general rule is 1 teaspoon of baking powder to 1 cup of flour. If the bread is heavy with fruit or nuts, or if it has much dark flour, use 1½ teaspoons per cup of flour. If several well-beaten eggs are used, less baking powder is necessary. If you have only single-acting baking powder on your shelf, follow the directions on the can. You will need more of the tartrate or phosphate baking powder than of the double-acting.

Be sure that your baking powder is fresh. If in doubt, test it by putting 1 teaspoon of powder in ½ cup of hot water. If it fizzes strongly it is all right to use.

Baking powder breads do not keep as long as yeast breads, but are delicious when fresh. They tend to dry out when frozen.

BAKING SODA

Baking soda is a chemical leavener used with sourdough, sour milk, or buttermilk. One-half teaspoon of soda to 1 cup of sourdough starter is the right amount; however, while making the sourdough bread lighter, the soda will also make it bland, with less of the authentic sourdough flavor. Use ½ to ¾ teaspoon baking soda to 1 cup of sour milk or buttermilk. For maximum leavening action, mix the soda with dry ingredients, not with the liquid. The soda must be thoroughly incorporated with the flour or the bread will be discolored and streaked.

BEATING

YEAST BREADS. Don't skimp on beating yeast breads, for this develops the gluten, which enables the dough to rise well, making a lighter bread. Use an electric mixer to beat in the first 2 cups of flour, which should be white if possible, setting at low speed for 1 minute, then increasing the speed to medium for 2 minutes. Stir in by hand enough of the remaining flour to make the dough roll away from the sides of the bowl. If you do not use an electric mixer, beat vigorously by hand for 300 strokes.

QUICK (BAKING POWDER) BREADS. Quick breads become tough with much beating. They should be mixed lightly and quickly, like muffins. Don't worry about the batter being lumpy. An overmixed quick bread will be full of holes and tunnels.

CARAMEL

Caramel, which is used in bread making for coloring rather than for flavor, is burned until it is bitter to the taste, though that is not noticeable in the bread. Put 1 cup of sugar and 1 tablespoon of water in a heavy skillet and cook over medium heat, stirring frequently, until it turns black and frothy. Add enough boiling water to make a heavy syrup. It will spatter when you add the water, so watch carefully. The sugar will coagulate into a ball when the water is added and must be melted over moderate heat until the syrup is smooth and of the right consistency. Cool and use what you need, bottling the rest for the next batch of dark bread. It will keep indefinitely.

COOLING

Yeast bread should be removed immediately from the pan and cooled on its side on a wire rack, to prevent sogginess. If you have baked in a fancy mold, let the bread stand for 5 minutes, sweet breads 10 to 15 minutes, for easier removal.

Allow quick breads to stay in the pans for 10 to 15 minutes after removing them from the oven, then turn out and cool on a rack.

CRUST

(Also see "Glazes")

For a good dark crust, use old, dark tin pans, glass, or dull aluminum. Glass makes a thick crust and the oven should be turned 25 degrees lower than called for in the recipe. For a very crisp crust like French bread, brush the loaf with cold water before baking and place a pan of hot water on the floor of the oven. If you want a soft crust (heaven forbid!), cover the bread with a clean dish towel while cooling.

DIETS, SPECIAL

SALT FREE. Substitute an equal amount of Adolph's Salt Substitute for the salt called for in the recipe. For dark breads use the seasoned salt substitute.

HIGH PROTEIN. To any given recipe, add ¼ cup of raw wheat germ and/or soya flour and ¼ cup powdered milk (do not reconstitute) per loaf, reducing the amount of flour accordingly. Or use the Cornell formula, adding 1 teaspoon of raw wheat germ, 1 tablespoon of soya flour, and 1 tablespoon of powdered milk to each cup of white flour.

LOW CALORIE. Substitute water for milk, omit shortening and sweetening, and use only ½ teaspoon of sugar in water when dissolving the yeast.

EGG ALLERGY. Substitute 1 tablespoon of lecithin for 1 egg, but do not use more than 2 tablespoons per recipe.

DAIRY PRODUCTS ALLERGY. Substitute water, broth, potato or rice water, or fruit juice for milk or cream. Use vegetable oil in place of butter.

CHOCOLATE ALLERGY. Substitute carob powder for chocolate.

GLUTEN OR WHEAT ALLERGY. Omit all wheat flour, substituting rye, buckwheat, or rice flours. This is tricky, for it is the gluten that makes a loaf light.

DONENESS

Bread is approaching doneness when it gives off that delicious, new bread fragrance.

Yeast or sourdough bread is done when the bread is a fine brown and has begun to shrink from the sides of the pan, though it will not pull away as much as a cake will. Turn the bread out of the pan and thump the bottom with your fingers. If it sounds hollow, it is done; if it doesn't, return the loaf to the pan and bake a little longer. If the loaf seems too soft when taken out of the pan, it may be placed on a cookie sheet or a piece of aluminum foil and baked another 5 minutes, or until it feels firm to the touch. If the top is already sufficiently brown, cover with a piece of foil.

If you are undecided whether the loaf has been baked long enough, insert a wooden skewer or toothpick into the center of the loaf. If it comes out clean, the bread is done. If not, return to the oven for another 5 minutes.

Quick bread is done when it is nicely browned and has shrunk away from the sides of the pan, and when a toothpick inserted in the middle comes out clean.

EGGS

The addition of one or more eggs will make bread lighter and more delicate, giving it a golden color, enriching the dough, and improving its character. The eggs should be at room temperature, or for greater volume, slightly warmed. Large eggs were used in the recipes in this book.

In yeast breads two large well-beaten eggs will require an additional ¾ cup of flour, or else ½ cup less liquid.

For a delicate quick bread, beat yolks and whites separately. Beat the whites until *dry* and fold in gently. This is contrary to all culinary advice but the dry whites will hold up better and therefore make a lighter loaf. Quick breads tend to be heavier than those made with yeast.

FILLINGS

Apricot

Combine 1 cup of apricot jam, ¼ cup chopped almonds, and 1 teaspoon cornstarch mixed into 1 tablespoon melted butter. Cook mixture over low heat until it thickens. If the jam is very thin, use 2 teaspoons of cornstarch. Cool before using.

Cinnamon Sugar

Spread rolled-out dough with soft butter and sprinkle generously with cinnamon sugar.

Cream Cheese

Soften 1 8-ounce package of cream cheese with a little milk to spreadable consistency. Add the grated rind of 1 lemon and 2 tablespoons sugar.

Date

1 cup chopped dates
½ cup water
1½ TBS. flour

½ cup sugar
Juice of ½ lemon
Dash of salt

Mix flour with the water and combine all ingredients. Cook until thick and cool before using.

Peach

Combine 1 cup peach jam, ¼ cup chopped almonds, and 1 teaspoon of cornstarch that has been mixed into 1 tablespoon melted butter. Cook over low heat until it thickens, and cool before using. If the jam is very thin, use 2 teaspoons of cornstarch.

Pecan

Cream ¼ cup butter and ¼ cup sugar until light. Add ¼ cup finely chopped or ground pecans and ½ teaspoon cinnamon.

14

Poppy Seed

1 cup poppy seeds	½ cup raisins
¼ cup butter	4 TBS. heavy cream
½ cup honey	1½ tsp. grated orange
1 cup coarsely crushed almonds	or lemon peel

Pour boiling water over poppy seeds and let stand overnight. Drain on paper towels and grind in the blender. Cream butter and honey together, add other ingredients. Cook together several minutes until smooth. Let cool before using.

Prune

1 cup thick prune purée	1 TBS. lemon juice
¼ cup sugar	

Combine these ingredients and cook until mixture has thickened. Cool before using.

Raisin and Date

⅓ cup raisins	⅓ cup water
⅓ cup chopped dates	

Combine these ingredients and cook together until very soft. Purée while warm and cool before using.

FREEZING

Yeast breads freeze well, but quick breads tend to dry out and are much better if eaten when freshly baked.

Cool the bread and wrap well in either foil or plastic wrap; then place in a plastic freezer bag. The ordinary utility plastic bags are not heavy enough. Defrost on a wire rack in its wrappings.

If you plan to serve the bread hot, remove from the oven while it is still pale in color, but nearly done, and freeze as above. When ready to use unwrap the bread and defrost. Return the loaf to the pan it was baked in, and continue the baking process until it is nicely browned.

Bread should not be frozen for more than three months, as it will become dry and lose flavor.

Dough may be frozen, but not for more than four weeks. Shape the dough into loaves and place in greased pans, allowing it to nearly complete the second rising. Freeze in the pans, to retain shape. When frozen remove from the pans and wrap well in plastic wrap or foil; place in a freezer bag, labeling with date and kind of bread. When you wish to bake it, place in a greased pan of the same size and defrost. Let the dough complete its second rising and bake according to the recipe. Allow plenty of time for this step; it may take the better part of the day.

FROSTINGS

(Also see "Glazes" and "Toppings")

These are used on sweet and festive breads. They are placed on top of the loaves after they are baked, while still warm.

Lemon or Orange Frosting

Mix the juice and grated rind of 2 lemons or 1 large orange with 1 cup of sifted confectioner's sugar and pour over the loaves as soon as they come out of the oven. Prick loaves with a fork so that the juice will penetrate. Cool in the pans for 10 minutes and then turn out on a wire rack to finish cooling.

Powdered Sugar Frosting

Brush the hot loaf with melted butter and dust generously with sifted confectioner's sugar. For a special flavor, keep a vanilla bean or a rose geranium leaf in a jar with the sugar.

16

White Frosting

Beat together 1 cup sifted confectioner's sugar with 2 tablespoons of either milk, cream, brandy, or rum. Drizzle this over the warm bread and let run down the sides. Almonds and candied cherries may be added immediately for a gay holiday touch.

If you wish a thicker, less runny frosting, let the loaf cool before frosting.

FRUIT

Fresh and dried fruits are delicious in breads. They are usually used in quick breads, but be sure to experiment with them in festive yeast breads also. Any of the following may be used separately or in combination. The amounts given are for one loaf.

- ½ to 1 cup raisins, either dark or light

- ¼ cup chopped candied orange or lemon rind; if freshly grated, use the rind of 1 orange or lemon

- ¼ cup chopped candied citron or cherries

- ½ cup puréed fruit—apricots, prunes, peaches, thick applesauce, etc.; if the purée is soupy, reduce liquid by the same amount

- ½ to 1 cup chopped dried, cooked fruit—apricots, prunes or peaches

- ¼ cup chopped raw apple; this may be grated, using the coarsest side of the grater

- 1 banana, crushed with a silver fork

- Juice of an orange or lemon; measure the amount and subtract it from the liquid called for in the recipe

GLAZES

(*See also "Frostings" and "Toppings"*)

Glazes are brushed on dough just before baking to give a loaf a rich color and a very professional look, and as a base to which sugar, nuts and seeds adhere. Use either a pastry brush or your fingers to apply.

- For a shiny, medium brown crust, brush with a yolk of egg beaten in 1 tablespoon water or milk.

- For a shiny crust with little browning, brush with white of egg beaten in 1 tablespoon water. For maximum shine, brush this on 5 minutes before the bread is done and return to the oven.

- A very dark glaze, good for black bread or any dark bread, is made with 1 teaspoon of Postum or instant coffee dissolved in 2 teaspoons of water.

- Milk used alone will give a smooth, even, and shiny crust.

- Melted butter brushed on when the loaf is removed from the oven will give it a rich appearance and will soften the crust.

- Honey and orange; combine ¼ cup honey with ½ cup orange juice.

- Sherry, for sweet breads; blend together 1½ cups powdered sugar, 2 tablespoons cream sherry, and 1 tablespoon each water and melted butter.

GLUTEN

Gluten is a protein substance which forms when the flour is moistened. It is found in wheat flour, and to a much lesser extent in rye. Gluten gives the dough elasticity and traps the carbon dioxide formed by yeast, making the dough rise. Flours other than white and whole wheat need to have wheat flour added for this reason. Hard beating after adding the wheat flour develops the gluten, as does kneading, making the bread lighter.

HERBS

(Also see "Spices")

Herbs and seeds greatly enhance a loaf of bread and should not be overlooked. These breads are particularly good with soups and salads. When baked in small pans (see "Utensils") they are perfect with cocktails. You will find many ideas for the use of herbs here, but experiment also with mixing herbs and using others not given here.

A year is the outside limit for keeping dried herbs, for they lose their color and flavor. Seeds may be kept twice as long. They should all be stored in light-proof and air-proof containers and kept away from heat. Fresh herbs from your own garden are the best of all. Use twice the amount if they are fresh, or more to your taste, as they become more pungent when dried.

Caraway Seeds

Caraway is much used in rye bread and good also in whole wheat. Use 1 teaspoon to 1 tablespoon per loaf, according to taste. It may also be sprinkled over a loaf that has been glazed with egg white and water (see "Glazes") before baking. Crush seeds with mortar and pestle when incorporating them into the dough. Cumin seeds may be substituted for caraway.

Celery Seeds

One tablespoon worked into the dough is enough for one loaf. Use 1 teaspoon for one of the little cocktail loaves. Sprinkle some seeds, before baking, on the top of a loaf which has been glazed with egg white and water (see "Glazes"), pressing them gently into the loaf.

Chives

Chives are very good in cocktail breads and cheese breads and go well with an equal amount of parsley, ¼ to ½ cup freshly picked and chopped. We do not recommend either of these herbs dried, as they lose their flavor.

Coriander

Crushed or ground coriander seed may be added to holiday breads to give a spicy flavor, which will be stronger if crushed. Use 1 teaspoon to 1 tablespoon per loaf.

Cumin Seeds

For those who do not like caraway seeds, cumin is a good substitute. It gives a delicious flavor to whole wheat and rye breads. Crush the seed with a mortar and pestle and use ½ to 1½ teaspoons per loaf, depending on how strong a flavor you wish. It may also be sprinkled, uncrushed, on top of a loaf that has been glazed with egg white and water (see "Glazes").

Dill Weed and Seed

Dill weed should be used fresh and is wonderful in a white batter bread or in a cheese loaf. It makes a delightful combination with fresh parsley. Use ¼ cup chopped fresh dill weed per loaf. Since dried dill weed does not hold its flavor well, dill seed may be substituted, 2 teaspoons crushed seed per loaf.

Fennel Seeds

Fennel has a licorice flavor, much like anise, but not so strong. It may be substituted for anise. Crush the seed with mortar and pestle before incorporating in the dough. The whole seeds may be used as a topping. Use ½ to 1½ teaspoons fennel per loaf.

Garlic

There is nothing better than garlic bread with salad. Add 1 to 2 cloves of garlic, peeled and finely minced, to a loaf, or ¼ to ½ teaspoon of reconstituted, dehydrated minced garlic, depending on how addicted to garlic you are. Try garlic juice added to softened butter and spread on French bread which has been sliced nearly through, spreading the butter between each slice and heating it before serving.

Marjoram

Marjoram mixes well with sage and thyme for a delicious whole wheat herb bread. See "Sage" for amounts.

Parsley

Parsley is delicious in a white or cheese bread, and blends with either chives or dill. Use ½ cup of fresh chopped parsley per loaf. The dried parsley does not have enough flavor to come through.

Poppy Seeds

These are usually sprinkled on top of a loaf or on rolls which have first been glazed with an egg white and water glaze (see "Glazes"). Poppy seeds may also be incorporated into the dough or used in a filling (see "Fillings"). If the seeds are used in the dough, mix in with the flour. Use ½ cup for a large loaf.

Rosemary

Mix 2 teaspoons of crushed dried rosemary with ¼ pound (1 stick) of soft butter. Slice a loaf of French bread almost to the bottom, spread the rosemary butter between the slices and heat. Magnificent! Rosemary may also be added to white dough, at the rate of 1½ teaspoons to 1 tablespoon if dried—and be sure to crush the leaves—or 2 tablespoons of fresh, finely chopped leaves.

Sage

For a fragrant whole wheat bread, mix dried sage, thyme, and marjoram, about ½ teaspoon of each, for 1 large loaf. If you are using fresh herbs, chop very fine, using 1½ to 2 teaspoons of each.

Sesame (Benne) Seeds

These seeds give a delightful nutty flavor to a loaf of bread. They may be used whole or ground, and as a topping or incorporated into the dough. Use 1 tablespoon to ¼ cup per loaf, according to taste. The seeds are easily ground in a blender, or with mortar and pestle; grinding increases the flavor, so use a smaller amount. When using them as a topping, glaze the loaf just before baking with an egg yolk or white beaten into 1 tablespoon of milk and sprinkle with the seeds, pressing them gently into the dough.

Thyme

Mix with sage and marjoram for a different whole wheat bread. See "Sage" for amounts.

Vanilla Beans

Keep a couple of vanilla beans in a can of sugar to use in delicate sweet yeast breads. And keep one in a jar of powdered sugar to sprinkle on tea loaves or coffee breads.

HIGH-ALTITUDE BAKING

YEAST BREADS. The rising period is shorter in high altitudes, resulting in diminished flavor. Punching down dough twice in the bowl before placing in pans to rise will develop better flavor by lengthening the rising time. Slower rising may also be accomplished by using less yeast. Watch the dough carefully to prevent overproofing. Also, since flour tends to dry out at high altitudes, more liquid may be needed.

QUICK BREADS. It may be necessary to slightly decrease the amount of baking powder in high altitudes. The Cooperative Extension Service of Colorado State College, Fort Collins, Colorado 80521, has an excellent bulletin #526S, "Making Yeast Breads at High Altitudes," 26 cents a copy, and Pamphlet #41, "High Altitude Food Preparations," which is free.

KNEADING

Dough is kneaded to develop the gluten, making it rise well and producing a bread that is lighter and finer textured than unkneaded bread, in which the gluten is developed entirely by beating.

Use a good-sized bread board and keep it for making bread only. Place it on a counter that is a comfortable height for working. A board measuring 16 inches by 22 inches, placed with its long side perpendicular to the edge of the counter, is the right size to reach to the back of the average counter so it will not slip as you knead. If you use a smaller board, a wet towel placed underneath will keep the board in place.

Flour the board and turn the dough out onto it. With floured hands, fold the back of the dough toward you, and with your palms push the dough away from you with a rolling motion. Give the dough a quarter turn and repeat, folding toward you and rolling away, adding only enough flour to the board to prevent the dough from sticking. If the dough is a very sticky one, place a canvas pastry cloth on top of your board and butter your hands. Kneading is a gentle process and not the time for working off one's frustrations. Knead lightly and rhythmically and you will feel better, and so will the dough. Continue to knead until the dough is bouncy and elastic and air bubbles are visible under the surface. At this point the dough will no longer be sticky. This will take about 10 minutes.

Too little kneading will give coarse bread of low volume. Bread is sufficiently kneaded when the indentation formed by sticking a finger into the dough springs back. Rich, sweet breads require less kneading.

A marble slab makes an excellent bread board and cuts down the time spent in kneading.

LECITHIN

Lecithin is a substance found in the human body. In its commercial form it is extracted from soy beans. It is high in protein, rich in phosphorus, and may be substituted for eggs if a person is allergic to them. Use 1 tablespoon of lecithin in place of each egg but not more than 2 tablespoons per recipe. One tablespoon per loaf may be used as a dough conditioner; it will make the texture more delicate and tender and is a natural preservative. Lecithin also acts as an emulsifier, breaking down fats, thus enabling the body to rid itself of excess cholesterol. It may be purchased in health food stores.

LIQUIDS

Water, potato water, rice water, milk, buttermilk, sour milk, fresh or sour cream, vegetable or meat broth, or fruit juices may all be used in making bread. Experiment with them for different flavors and textures. Water gives a crisper and crustier loaf, but the bread will dry out more rapidly unless you add a generous amount of fat. If your water is very soft you will need less yeast. Dough made with alkaline water is a slow riser and needs another tablespoon of yeast. Potato water produces a fast-rising bread. Any type of milk or cream makes a rich, fine-textured loaf.

In making up your own yeast recipes, a good rule of thumb is to use one part of liquid to three of flour per loaf. Reduce the amount of liquid if you are using many eggs or other liquids such as oil or syrup. No need to keep liquid measurements exact, but remember to keep proportions of liquid to flour in balance. Too much liquid results in soggy bread, while too little will make it dry.

In making quick breads, use approximately 1½ to 2 cups of liquid to 3 cups of flour per loaf. Measurements are not as critical in yeast breads as they are in quick breads and cakes.

MEASURE-MENTS

All measurements in this book are level. Pack brown sugar when measuring.

MILK

Milk will give bread a softer and finer, more cakelike texture, and a delicate flavor. The crust will be thinner and softer than that of bread made with water.

Milk should be hot (see "Temperatures"), but need not be scalded if you are using pasteurized milk. Unpasteurized milk *must* be scalded, not boiled, to kill enzymes that inhibit yeast action. However, in making sweet breads, scalding will produce a more delicate bread. When making quick breads use lukewarm milk. If you are scalding milk, rinse the saucepan first in cold water, for easier cleaning.

Dry skim milk may be substituted and need not be scalded or reconstituted. Just use warm water and add the dry milk to the flour. This is particularly good for use in low calorie bread or as a fortifier of regular milk for higher nutritional value.

Sour milk, sour cream, buttermilk, and yogurt all give bread an interesting flavor and a very fine, delicate texture. Use ½ teaspoon baking soda per cup of sour milk or cream. Mix it into the flour thoroughly, or the bread will be streaky. For an acceptable substitute for sour milk or sour cream, or for buttermilk, add 1½ tablespoons of lemon juice or 1¼ tablespoons of vinegar to each cup of warm sweet milk or cream and let stand for a few minutes.

OIL

Oil used as a shortening results in a rich, cakelike bread. Any cooking oil will do, but do not use olive oil, for it is too rich and has too heavy a flavor. Peanut oil gives a distinctive flavor. Sesame oil has a nutty flavor and is particularly good with dark flours. However, it is polysaturated and not for those on a low-cholesterol diet. Sesame oil should be kept refrigerated.

For refrigerator-rise breads, use oil as shortening for greater volume.

OVENS

Ovens differ so much that it is hard to give specific directions for baking temperatures. It is very important always to use a good oven thermometer in order to know your oven's idiosyncracies.

Preheat at least 15 minutes before baking, for minimum fluctuation and maximum accuracy.

If your bread rises higher on one side than the other, you have a hot spot in your oven. For even, well-shaped loaves, place the pans on the diagonal. This will permit a more even circulation of heat, thus minimizing the effect of the hot spot.

To make good French bread, it is necessary to approximate a French oven. This can easily be done by using either quarry tile or Johns Manville's Colorlith, both of which may be found at any large yard that carries building construction supplies. The tiles may be fitted together on the middle rack in the oven. Colorlith must be ground smooth. With either material there must be a two-inch free space to the oven walls so that the heat may circulate. When the material is in place, preheat the oven for 20 minutes, then place a pan of boiling water on the lowest rack of an electric oven or on the floor of a gas one. Dust the tiles or Colorlith generously with cornmeal and slide the loaves, which have risen on a cookie sheet also generously dusted with cornmeal, onto them with a little jerk. Once they are on the tiles it is impossible to move them for several minutes, so be careful of your aim. Brush the loaves with water several times during baking, or if you have a plant mister, spray them. This gives the thick, crisp crust of French bread.

REHEATING

To reheat bread or rolls, sprinkle the inside of a brown paper bag with water and shake out. Place bread or rolls inside, close, and heat in a hot oven set at 350° for 10 to 15 minutes, according to size. They will not dry out if reheated in this way.

RISING

When your dough is ready for its first rising, form it into a ball and place, smooth side down, in a large, well-greased bread bowl; then turn the ball so that the greased side is up, to prevent a crust forming. A crust that is dry and inelastic prevents the dough from expanding. Cover with greased plastic wrap or wax paper and add a folded dish towel for warmth. Put in a warm place out of drafts, in a temperature of 70° to 85°. Too hot an area will kill the yeast, and too cold will inhibit rising. We find that the best place is in the oven. In a gas oven the pilot light will give just enough warmth; if the oven is electric, turn the thermostat as low as possible and leave the heat on for a couple of seconds. If the element begins to turn red, the oven is too hot. Leaving the oven lights on during the rising period will maintain a gentle warmth.

Let the dough rise until it is double in bulk, or until the indentations formed by thrusting two fingers into the dough remain. First rising will take 1 to 2 hours for white bread and somewhat longer for dark breads. The length of time depends on warmth and humidity. Don't be disconcerted if the time varies. Never hurry the rising process, for slow rising allows the flavor to develop. This is particularly true for white bread, which otherwise will taste rather bland. Do not let your dough rise so high that it falls back on itself or you will have dry, coarse bread. If this should happen, knead for 5 minutes and allow it to rise again.

When the dough has risen sufficiently, turn it out on a floured board and knead again. Shape into loaves and place in the bread pans. Let rise again in a warm, draft-free place. This second rising will take less time than the first. Cover again as you did the first time, to prevent crusting.

If you are making unkneaded bread, punch the dough down with your fist when it has risen enough and stir it in the bowl for 25 strokes; then put in pans for the second rising.

French bread should rise three times in bulk instead of double, and it needs an extra rising, twice in the bowl and once after the loaves are formed. This develops its distinctive flavor.

Dough will rise slowly in the refrigerator. If you find that you are not going to have enough time to complete the whole process, this method will allow you to have controlled rising so you can bake when convenient during the day. After kneading—or, if making un-kneaded bread, after mixing—let the covered dough rise for 20 minutes, form loaves and place the dough in pans. Cover loosely with waxed paper, add plastic, and put in the refrigerator for from 2 to 24 hours. When you are ready to bake, let stand in a warm room for 15 minutes, while the oven is preheating.

If the dough has not had enough rising time, the bread will be dry and irregular in texture, and small in volume. Slightly overrisen bread will produce excessive volume and will crumble when it is cut. Bread that has risen too much will be full of large holes and will have a rough-textured crust. Also it may fall and so should be kneaded and allowed to rise again.

After the loaves are shaped and have risen in the pans, a gentle touch with a finger will leave a light indentation when they are ready for baking.

SALT

Salt is a most useful ingredient in bread; it does much more than just keep bread from tasting flat. It prevents yeast from working too fast, thus giving good flavor and good volume without overdeveloping the gluten, and it also keeps the bread moist. Since it retards fermenta-tion, it is most helpful in warm weather, when dough is apt to rise too quickly; use a little more salt on very warm days. Too much salt, however, will inhibit the rising action of yeast.

In white bread, 1 teaspoon per loaf is about right, but 1½ teaspoons will be needed in bread made from cereals or dark flours.

Too little salt softens the dough and makes it sticky, and crumbly when the loaf is cut. Rolls and sweet breads need less salt than regular breads because of the additional sugar present.

If you accidentally leave out the salt, sift it into the flour used in kneading and work it in thoroughly.

For those on a salt-free diet, substitute the same amount of Adolph's Salt Substitute. It won't be as tasty, but much better than without it.

SHORTENING

Shortening makes a loaf of bread moist, rich, and tender and adds flavor. Although butter gives the best flavor, margarine, white shortening, or vegetable oil may be used. Oil is preferable when making cool-rise breads. Lard is frequently used in country baking, but since it is highly polysaturated we do not recommend it.

One tablespoon of shortening per loaf is minimum. Up to a cup may be used for very rich, sweet breads. Dark flours require less shortening than white, for they contain the fatty portion of the whole grain. Breads having no shortening should be eaten immediately, as they quickly become dry.

SOURDOUGH

Sourdough bread, made with a fermented "starter" as a leavener instead of yeast, has been used since the Egyptians and has been the mainstay of pioneers and campers. It has a distinctive flavor and is delicious, though chewier and with less volume than conventional yeast bread. There are many different ways of making starters, each giving its own flavor to the bread.

SPICES

Spices, seeds, and herbs add greatly to the flavor of bread and give a festive touch to any loaf. Try them in everyday breads as well as holiday loaves.

Spices lose their flavor and should not be kept over a year, so buy in small quantities. Store in airtight containers and keep in a dark, cool place for maximum flavor. Seeds are more pungent if crushed with mortar and pestle or with a rolling pin.

Amounts given here may be varied according to taste. Experiment until you find the amount that pleases your palate.

Anise

Anise is a small seed with a delicate licorice taste. It should be crushed for added flavor. It is used in Christmas, Easter, and other festive breads. It is good in quick breads and in Greek loaves. Use 1½ teaspoons per loaf.

Cardamom

What would Christmas breads be without cardamom? It is the essence of holiday breads. You can also dress up an ordinary bread with it for a change of pace. Use 1 teaspoon either crushed or ground. We prefer to buy the whole seed, remove the outer cover, and grind the seed with mortar and pestle, since the flavor is better than in the commercially ground product.

Cinnamon

Cinnamon is a most useful and versatile spice for breakfast breads, coffee cakes, festive and holiday breads, and rolls. It is very good in rye bread instead of caraway. Try it in squash, pumpkin, or sweet potato breads for a different taste. Use 1 teaspoon per loaf.

Clove

This is a strong and pungent spice, so use sparingly in holiday breads. About ¼ teaspoon per loaf is right.

Ginger

Try this spice in pumpkin or squash bread. You will need ½ teaspoon per loaf.

Mace

Mace is not used in bread as much as it should be, for it has a lovely, elusive flavor. Use it in plain, whole wheat, or rye bread or in festive white breads. It is strong and ¼ teaspoon per loaf is enough. This is our favorite spice. Do try it!

Nutmeg

Use this spice sparingly for subtle flavor, and combine it with cinnamon in festive breads. For maximum flavor, freshly grate or grind a whole nutmeg. One-half teaspoon per loaf is sufficient.

Pepper

Freshly ground black pepper is delightful in a bread served with cocktails or with salads. Use ½ to ¾ teaspoon per loaf.

Saffron

Saffron is the most expensive spice in the world—and worth every penny that you pay for it. You need only a pinch of powdered saffron, or two or three threads. It should be used in white breads, where its delicate flavor will be at its best, such as in holiday breads and rolls.

SPONGE

A sponge is a batter consisting of half the flour, the dissolved and foaming yeast, and the water or milk called for in a recipe, mixed together well and allowed to rise for several hours or overnight. Though this method is a longer process, the additional rising time enhances the flavor of the bread. When the sponge is well risen (it generally takes at least three hours) stir in by hand the remaining ingredients called for in the recipe, and proceed according to directions.

We use the sponge method primarily in sourdough bread, allowing the starter to work overnight. Directions for making the sponge are given in each sourdough recipe in this book.

STARTER

Starter is the leavening agent in sourdough bread. In its simplest form it consists of a fermented mixture of water or milk, flour, and wild yeast. Other starters are more elaborate. There is a section on starters and starter recipes under "Sourdough Breads."

STORAGE

FLOUR. Ordinary commercial flour may be stored at room temperature and should be kept in a dark place.

The dark grains bought in health food shops and not commercially ground have not had the germ removed and therefore do not keep well. They should be bought in small quantities and kept in a cool, dry, dark place in airtight containers. A good method is to put them into clean, well-marked coffee cans and store in the refrigerator. If frozen, dark grains will keep indefinitely. With improper storage they quickly become rancid.

Always remember to bring refrigerated or frozen flour to room temperature before using. This is quickly accomplished in a warming oven.

BREAD. For long-term storage, freeze your bread (see "Freezing"). White bread being used should be well wrapped and kept at room temperature for maximum· moistness and flavor. It will keep about a week without becoming moldy. In the refrigerator it will not mold but it will dry out, even if well wrapped, and there will be a definite loss of flavor. However, dark breads will stay fresh longer if kept in the refrigerator. If you eat very little bread, it is better to cut a freshly baked loaf in two and freeze half.

SWEETENING

Some form of sweetening should be used in bread making, to give the yeast or starter food to work on and thus produce a lighter bread. Sugar, honey, maple syrup, or molasses are all good and are interchangeable in any recipe. Use 1 tablespoon to ½ cup of any of these per loaf. In sweet yeast breads or quick breads use up to 1 cup of sugar. In any bread, use a little less honey than granulated sugar if you wish to substitute.

Sugar physically modifies the gluten, giving dough of good consistency, with moist crumb and a good crust. Breads that have much sugar brown faster. Watch carefully as you bake, and cover with a foil tent when the loaf has reached a rich, golden color.

Brown sugar is easier to measure and to incorporate into the flour if it has been allowed to dry out and then is broken up with a rolling pin. But if you wish to keep it soft, put a few bread crusts in the jar with the sugar. If it is already hard and you wish to soften it, put in the oven at a very low temperature for 10 minutes.

WHITE BREADS. Granulated sugar may be used, but either honey or light brown sugar will give more flavor. Honey gives a delightful taste and also acts as a preservative, though it makes a slightly heavier loaf and it's sticky to knead. It is a must in Christmas breads.

DARK BREADS. These are good sweetened with dark brown sugar, dark molasses, strong dark honey, or maple syrup. We like the thick, very dark syrup, known as maple molasses, which is made from the last run of the sap. Cane molasses makes a heavy, chewy, moist, and very flavorful bread, very good with dark grains.

Do not use sweetening in French, country, or peasant types of bread, except the ½ teaspoon sugar needed when dissolving yeast.

Scandinavian pearl sugar is excellent for sprinkling on top of festive breads, or crush rock candy for a topping.

TEMPERA-TURES

FOR MIXING

Temperature is very important when using yeast, for high temperatures will kill it and low ones make it dormant. The Fleischmann Rapidmix method requires that all liquids be 120° to 130°, whereas the old-fashioned method requires 105° to 115°. It is not necessary to use a thermometer. For the old method, if a few drops on the inside of your wrist feel neither hot nor cold, the temperature is right. For Rapidmix, use water as hot as you can comfortably put your hand in. Compressed yeast calls for lukewarm water.

When making sourdough bread, in order not to kill the starter, have your liquids the same temperature as for the old-fashioned yeast method.

FOR RISING

Dough should rise in temperatures between 70° and 85° and in a draft-free place. The cooler the temperature the longer the rising time. At high altitudes, bread is apt to rise too fast, with resulting loss of flavor. Prolonging the time by having it rise in a cool place is advantageous.

For Baking

Yeast breads should be baked first at 375° to 400° for 10 minutes. If the oven heat is right, browning should not take place in that period. Then reduce the temperature to 350° to 325° for 25 to 40 minutes, depending on the recipe. If you like a very dark crust, use the upper figures.

Rich doughs, with generous amounts of sugar and butter, brown rapidly and must be carefully watched. Use a cooler oven, starting at 350°, and lower the temperature to 325° after 10 minutes. When the loaf is sufficiently brown but not thoroughly cooked, cover with a tent of aluminum foil.

Quick breads should bake more slowly and at lower temperatures than yeast breads, usually from 325° to 300°. They will take from 50 minutes to 1¼ hours.

TOPPINGS

Toppings are usually placed on top of the loaves before they are baked. They should be gently pressed into the dough.

Cinnamon

Five minutes before the bread is done remove from oven, glaze the loaf with melted butter, and sprinkle with cinnamon sugar. Return to oven and finish baking.

Crunch

A crunchy topping may be made by combining 2 tablespoons of butter with 4 tablespoons *each* of sugar and flour. Cinnamon may be added to this, according to taste.

Granola-Type Cereal
(without Raisins)

Mix together ⅓ cup of any granola-type cereal, rolling out the lumps, and 2 tablespoons of melted butter. This is a quick, easy, and slightly sweet topping, especially delicious with dark breads.

Rolled Oats

A loaf of oatmeal bread looks very pretty if it is glazed with melted butter and sprinkled with rolled oats, which must be gently pressed into the dough so that they will not fall off.

Seeds or Nuts

Seeds or nuts sprinkled over a loaf that has been glazed with the white of 1 egg beaten together with 1 tablespoon of water make an excellent topping. Use either celery, sesame, caraway, cumin, or poppy seeds, or any nuts chopped rather fine.

Sugar

Glaze the loaf with melted butter and sprinkle with pearl sugar or rock candy that has been hammered into very small pieces.

UTENSILS
Beg, borrow, or steal those awful-looking old, dark, much used tin bread pans. They give the bread a lovely brown crust. Lacking these, buy new pans of good quality and heavy weight. Before being used, they should be put in a hot oven until they lose their brightness. The new black steel pans are also good, giving a brown, crusty loaf. Bread

baked in Teflon pans does not brown well and we do not recommend them. Glass gives a very heavy crust and requires an oven 25 degrees cooler than called for in the recipe. A bright shiny aluminum pan does not brown well, but there are dull-finished aluminum pans on the market that are satisfactory, although not as good as the heavier pans. If your pans are very shiny, bake on the bottom shelf of your oven.

There are many sizes of pans on the market. A pan 9½ by 4½ by 2½ inches is a good average size. An 8½ by 4½ by 2½ inch pan is especially recommended by Fleischmann for their CoolRise bread (for more information on the CoolRise mixing methods, refer to "Mixing Methods"). A small pan, 5½ by 3 by 2 inches, is very nice for small loaves and will take a quarter of an average recipe. Children love these. We make our own very small pans, 8 by 2½ by 2 inches, from the heavy foil pans that frozen loaf cakes come in, by cutting one in half lengthwise with heavy scissors, telescoping the two halves to the above size, and stapling each end at the top and bottom, then rolling one rim over the other at each end and crimping. These make delightful little loaves for tea and cocktail breads.

Jelly molds, rings, fish molds, melon molds, casseroles, bundt pans are all fun to use and are particularly good for sweet breads and coffee cakes. Try various sizes of tin cans also.

A large earthen or pottery bread bowl of the old-fashioned variety is a necessity. The straighter the sides, the better the dough will rise.

An electric mixer is excellent for developing gluten in the beginning stages of bread making. Then you should switch to a wooden spoon or wooden paddle, easier on the hands than a metal one, and a must for sourdough, since metal will give the dough a metallic taste.

A bread mixer is available with a bread hook, which will do your kneading for you. Some electric mixers have a bread hook attachment. They will save time and energy and are expensive. We like to knead bread the old-fashioned way; we like to put our hands in a gooey mass and feel it come alive.

Get a good hardwood bread board and keep it just for kneading bread. A board 16 inches by 22 inches is a good size. Placed with the long side perpendicular to the edge of the counter, it will be braced by the back of the counter and so will not slip as you knead. Or place a wet cloth under the board to hold it in place. An old marble slab is an excellent substitute and cuts down the time spent in kneading.

A baker's scraper is very useful to keep the board clean as you knead, though a knife will do.

For a very light and delicate dough, use a pastry cloth, since less flour will be required to keep it from sticking. Sprinkle the cloth with flour and rub in before kneading. Shake the flour out well before storing the cloth.

VEGETABLES

Some vegetables make delicious additions to a loaf of bread. Experiment, but keep away from the cabbage family, which has too strong a flavor. Here are the ones that we like, with suggested amounts for *two* loaves.

Carrots

Grate raw carrots and let drain a few minutes. Use 1 cup.

Eggplant

Grate 2 cups of eggplant pulp, using the coarsest grater. It makes a very good quick bread and gives an unusual flavor.

Onion

Onion bread is excellent with salads or as a cocktail bread. Toasted, it is a fine base for a hamburger. One-half cup of fresh minced onion or ¼ cup of dehydrated minced onion added to the hot liquid gives two savory loaves.

For a slightly different flavor, try a package of Lipton's dehydrated soup added to the liquid when mixing dough.

Potato, Sweet

Use ½ to 1 cup of cooked, mashed potato, either fresh or canned.

Potato, White

One cup of mashed potato, made from either fresh or instant potatoes, makes a moist loaf and gives good volume. Keep the potato water and use in place of the liquid called for in the recipe.

Pumpkin

Use 1 cup of pumpkin, cooked and mashed, either fresh or canned.

Rice

Use 1 cup of cooked rice.

Squash, Winter

Use ³/₄ to 1 cup of cooked, mashed squash, fresh or frozen. If you use the frozen, defrost and drain well.

Zucchini

Grate coarsely and drain well, pressing gently to get rid of excess moisture. You will need 1 to 2 cups.

YEAST

A living microscopic fungus, yeast is the leavening agent in all yeast breads. It produces gas by converting sugar into carbon dioxide and alcohol, thus causing the dough to rise. It comes in two forms, compressed cake yeast, which is very perishable and will keep only a week in the refrigerator, or active dry yeast, which is dormant. The active dry yeast comes in dated package form or in bulk and may be kept in a cool place for about a year. For economy's sake, buy it in bulk. Fleischmann now packages it in 4-ounce jars, or it may be bought in health food stores. Opened jars must be refrigerated. Be sure to ask for baker's yeast, because brewer's yeast will give the bread a very disagreeable taste.

One cake of compressed yeast, or 1 envelope of active dry yeast, or 1 scant tablespoon of bulk yeast are all equivalent and are interchangeable in any recipe.

In Fleischmann's Rapidmix method, yeast may be mixed directly with the first two cups of flour. We prefer to keep to the time-honored way and proof for freshness, by dissolving it in ¼ cup of warm water with 1 teaspoon sugar for about 5 minutes. If the yeast becomes frothy and increases in volume, it is active.

Temperature is important with yeast, for it is killed by high temperatures and is inactive at low ones. See "Temperatures" for degrees of heat.

A two-loaf batch of white bread needs 1 tablespoon of yeast. For very rich white breads, or for whole wheat and dark, heavy flours which contain less gluten, and for all stone-ground ones, 2 to 3 tablespoons of yeast are necessary, depending on the ratio of dark flour to white. We recommend not using more than 1 tablespoon of yeast for 2 loaves in very hot weather, since otherwise the dough will rise too fast resulting in a less flavorful loaf.

If your bread refuses to rise properly, dissolve more yeast with sugar in a small amount of water and knead into the dough. Let rise again.

If you wish to halve a recipe calling for 1 tablespoon of yeast, use the whole amount of yeast and the water in which it is dissolved as called for in the recipe and halve the remaining ingredients. But if it calls for 2 tablespoons of yeast, you may halve that amount, using 1 tablespoon. Do not halve the amount of water it is dissolved in. If you plan to double a recipe calling for 2 tablespoons of yeast, use 3 tablespoons, not 4.

All recipes in this book were tested with active dry yeast.

YOGURT

One-half cup of yogurt mixed with ½ cup of either whole or skim milk gives a nice tang to a loaf of bread.

—

3 Flours and Cereals

FLOURS

A loaf of bread is no better than the materials that go into it, and though the best flours will cost a little more, they are well worth it. The fresh, stone-ground flours found in health food stores are very good, for they have not been subjected to the high heat generated by modern high-speed machinery which damages the flavor. They require more yeast than commercial grinds.

In whole flour, the grain has been ground without removing any of its parts, such as the germ embryo and bran. Whole flour therefore has better flavor and more vitamins. But because the germ has not been removed, the flour does not keep as well as commercial types found on supermarket shelves. Buy in small quantities and keep in a cool, dark place, in an airtight container, or in the freezer, where it will keep a long time. But remember that frozen flour will inhibit yeast action, so the flour must be brought to room temperature. This can quickly be accomplished in a warming oven.

White flour is high in gluten, a protein substance found in wheat flour, and to a lesser extent in rye. It gives the dough elasticity, developed as the dough is beaten and kneaded, and traps the gases formed by the yeast, causing the dough to rise. For this reason, wheat flour should be mixed with other grains which do not contain gluten.

Experiment with blending various flours together, varying the amount and kind. Whole wheat flour may be used without the addition of white flour, making a very dense loaf of the European type, but rye, barley, corn, and others should be combined with white flour. They are either too sticky or too heavy when used alone. A good rule is to start with 2 cups of dark flour to 4 of white. Next time you may use either more or less, according to taste. In substituting dark flour for white in any recipe, use about $7/8$ cup of dark in place of 1 cup of white.

Recipes in this book have been tested with unbleached, pre-sifted, all-purpose flour, because of its better flavor and high gluten content. We used King Arthur Flour or Hecker's but Pillsbury also has an unbleached flour on the market now. Self-rising flours are not desirable since they contain baking powder and soda, which are not necessary with yeast and sourdough. Since different mills produce flour containing varying amounts of gluten, and since flour is also affected by weather conditions which change the consistency of the dough, it is impossible to give definite amounts. With a little experience one can tell by the feel if enough flour has been added.

Meals are more coarsely ground than flours of the same grain.

Barley

Barley makes a moist, sweet, fine-textured bread. It contains no gluten and therefore must be mixed with white flour, in at least equal parts. Try it lightly pan-toasted. The toasting must be very light or the flour will have a bitter flavor. The Germans use barley flour in their black bread.

Amount per loaf: ½ to 1 cup.

44

Bran

Bran is the outer covering of the wheat kernel and is either ground with the whole wheat or removed and ground separately. It has a pleasant taste and gives the bread good texture. It also provides roughage.

Amount per loaf: ¼ to ½ cup.

Buckwheat

Since buckwheat has a high fat content, both the flour and the groats must be fresh. Keep it in your freezer. The flavor of buckwheat is distinctive, making interesting bread and pancakes. In Germany it is used in black bread. Since it has no gluten, it should be mixed with white flour. It may be used in its natural form, which has a more delicate flavor but makes a heavier bread, or you may use dark buckwheat, which, having been toasted, has a stronger taste.

Amount per loaf: ¼ to 1 cup.

Buckwheat Groats (Kasha)

This is the whole kernel with the outer husks removed. It is rich in protein and minerals and is a good source of B vitamins. It may be used either raw or cooked, though we prefer the raw. It gives bread a pleasant, nutty flavor and good texture. To cook, use two parts of water to one part of groats and cook for 20 minutes.

Amount per loaf: ¼ to ½ cup uncooked; ½ to 1 cup cooked.

Carob

The flour is made from the edible pod of the carob, an ever-green tree of the Mediterranean area. The pod is sometimes called St. John's Bread. (Don't fail to try this delicate carob tea bread found in the chapter on "Quick Breads.")

The flour may be bought either plain or toasted. Toasted carob tastes like chocolate and as such is a boon to those who are allergic to chocolate; it is also much lower in fat content and high in protein. Carob flour may be substituted in the same proportion as cocoa in a cake or sweet bread. If you are substituting for chocolate, 3 table-spoons of carob flour and 1½ teaspoons of fat (i.e., butter or margarine) should be used for 1 square (1 ounce) of chocolate.

Amount per loaf: ½ cup.

Cornell Triple-Rich Formula

This nourishing formula for enriching white flour was developed at Cornell University for high-protein bread. Place 1 tablespoon each of skim milk powder and soya flour and 1 teaspoon of raw wheat germ in a one cup measure and fill with white flour. Use in place of the white flour specified in any recipe.

Cornmeal

Either yellow or white cornmeal may be used. The stone-ground makes a coarser bread. Since it lacks gluten, it makes a very heavy loaf by itself and should be mixed with wheat flour. A couple of tablespoons added to the flour in white bread gives a crunchy and crumbly texture that is very pleasant.

Amount per loaf: 2 tablespoons to 1 cup uncooked; ½ cup cornmeal mush.

46

Gluten

This is the protein substance in whole wheat grain and is what gives the elasticity to dough. The flour, having had a large part of the starch removed, is 40 percent protein and therefore makes a good diet bread. It may be used with white flour or with whole grain flours low in gluten, such as rye.

Amount per loaf: ½ to 2 cups.

Graham

Graham flour is whole wheat finely milled by a special process, which gives it its delicate and different flavor. It makes a lighter bread than whole wheat flour. While it is interchangeable with whole wheat in any recipe, it will not taste the same. It is hard to find and many health food stores will tell you that it is the same as whole wheat, but don't be misled. It is very good combined with buttermilk and is one of our favorite flours. Be sure to try it.

Amount per loaf: ½ to 2 cups.

Kasha

(See "Buckwheat Groats")

Oat Flour

This is finely ground from the whole oat kernel and should be mixed with white or whole wheat flours. It may easily be ground at home by placing rolled oats in your blender and whirling till fine. It makes a very delicate bread.

Amount per loaf: ½ to 1½ cups.

Oatmeal (Rolled Oats)

Oatmeal may be used raw or cooked and makes a very good, moist, and rather sweet bread that is rich in minerals and proteins. It contains no gluten, so must be used with wheat flour. Either old-fashioned or quick rolled oats may be used, though the former gives greater flavor. Instant oatmeal is not recommended since it lacks flavor. Oatmeal needs more salt than most cereals, at least 1 tablespoon for two loaves.

Amount per loaf: ½ to 1½ cups raw; ½ to ¾ cup cooked.

Potato Flour

Potato flour makes a very dense loaf and must be mixed with white flour. The bread will be moist and long-keeping.

Amount per loaf: ¼ to ½ cup.

Rice Flour, Brown

This flour produces dark, heavy, moist, and rather sweet bread when used alone. For a light and delicate loaf it should be mixed with white flour, but it will make a satisfactory substitute for wheat flour for those allergic to wheat. Cooked brown rice gives bread a chewy consistency.

Amount per loaf: ½ cup upwards raw; ½ cup cooked.

Rye

Rye is the only flour besides wheat to contain gluten. However the gluten content is low and it needs wheat to provide elasticity.

Used alone it is difficult to handle, though it will be fine-textured and moist. For a light rye use 1 cup of rye to 5 cups of white flour to make two loaves, and for a dark rye use 3 cups of rye to 3 cups of white flour. The more rye you use, the lower the volume. There are two kinds of rye flour, light and dark, but the dark is very difficult to find. Rye is a good substitute for those with wheat allergies.

Amount per loaf: ½ cup for light rye and 1½ cups for dark rye.

Soya (or Soy)

Soya is a highly concentrated protein, lacking gluten and starch. It is fifteen times as rich in calcium and ten times as rich in iron as wheat flour. It gives a delightful flavor if used in small proportions, not more than 1 cup to 5 cups of other flours. When making whole wheat bread try 2 tablespoons of soya to each cup of whole wheat. It contains considerable fat, so use a moderate amount of shortening. Soya flour makes a bouncy dough which rises well and produces a delicate, light loaf, though too much of it will make the bread heavy. Cover the loaves with aluminum foil after the first 15 minutes of baking, as it browns very quickly. Bread containing soya keeps well, but the flour should be kept under refrigeration.

Amount per loaf: ¼ to ½ cup.

Wheat, Cracked

Cracked wheat is a very coarsely ground whole wheat flour. It gives the bread a crunchy texture and a rather different flavor from the regular grind.

Amount per loaf: ½ to 1½ cups.

Wheat Germ

This is very high in protein and minerals. Up to ½ cup may be added to any loaf for extra nourishment. We use it in its raw form in the recipes in this book, but it may be pan-toasted for a nuttier flavor. In any form it gives bread a special flavor.

Amount per loaf: ¼ to ½ cup.

Wheat, White

All-purpose unbleached white flour is a combination of hard and soft wheat with the bran removed. It has good flavor and is high in gluten. It is a necessary component of any bread made of dark flours.

Amount per loaf: 2½ to 3½ cups for white bread; ½ to 2 cups in combination with whole grains.

Wheat, Whole

This is made from the whole grain, bran, germ, and all, and it makes a dark and flavorful bread. Mix it with white flour for a finer-textured and lighter loaf. It is very absorbent and so requires less liquid than white flour does. It is high in protein (containing 40 percent) and in gluten.

Amount per loaf: ½ to 2 cups.

Wheat, Whole—Pastry Flour

This is not suitable for yeast breads but is excellent in quick breads (and of course pastry), making a lighter loaf. It may be substituted for whole wheat flour but will have somewhat less flavor.

Amount per loaf: ½ to 3 cups.

BREAKFAST CEREALS

Breakfast cereals make a real contribution to breads and give a wide variation in flavor. Either dry or cooked cereals may be used. Be sure to experiment with both types of cereals. When added to flours, they make delicious breads with interesting flavor. There are several excellent recipes calling for cereals in this book. A good rule of thumb is to use 1½ cups of uncooked cereal in place of 1 cup of flour.

Bran Flakes

This is coarse and can be added for texture and flavor.

Amount per loaf: ½ cup.

Granola

This makes delicious bread, but eat it up fast, as it loses flavor very quickly.

Amount per loaf: ½ to 1 cup.

Maltex

This is a blend of wheat and barley and is particularly good when used with part barley flour.

Amount per loaf: ½ to 1 cup uncooked.

Quaker 100% Natural Cereal

This is delicious and, since it is rather sweet, is best used in a sweet loaf, either yeast or baking powder. It also makes a fine topping for oatmeal bread. Refer to "Toppings" under "Tips, Terms, and Ingredients."

Amount per loaf: ½ to 1 cup.

Ralston

Ralston is a whole wheat cereal with some wheat germ added. Try it with ¼ teaspoon of mace.

Amount per loaf: ¼ to ¾ cup uncooked.

Roman Meal

This is a fine mixed bag of wheat, rye, bran, flaxseed, wheat germ, and rye germ and is one of the best for flavor.

Amount per loaf: ½ to ¾ cup uncooked.

Samp Cereal

This is a stone-ground cereal, half crushed corn and half crushed wheat. It makes a delicious bread (and try it as a breakfast cereal also). It can be purchased from the Vermont Craftsmen, Inc. in the list of suppliers.

Amount per loaf: ½ cup uncooked.

Shredded Wheat

Use with white flour for unusual flavor.

Amount per loaf: 1 to 3 pieces.

Wheatena

Your loaf of bread will taste like cooked Wheatena.

Amount per loaf: ½ to ¾ cup uncooked.

Wheatsels

Another mixed bag of whole wheat, oats, corn, soya, and honey. And it makes mighty good bread. Wheatsels can be purchased from Walnut Acres, also in the list of suppliers.

Amount per loaf: ½ cup.

SUPPLIERS

The following list will give you excellent sources from which you can purchase the cereals and many of the flours mentioned in this chapter.

- Elmolino Mills
  345 North Baldwin Park Boulevard
  Industry, California 91746

- Erewhon Trading Co.
  33 Farnsworth Street
  Boston, Massachusetts 02210

- Good Earth Natural Foods
  1336 First Avenue
  New York, New York 10021

- Great Valley Mills
  Quakertown, Pennsylvania 18951

- Lekvar-by-the-Barrell
  H. Roth & Son Paprika Co.
  1577 First Avenue
  New York, New York 10028

- The Vermont Craftsmen, Inc.
  Weston, Vermont 05161

- Walnut Acres
  Penns Creek, Pennsylvania 17862

You can also look in the yellow pages for the names of health food stores near you.

4 Mixing Methods

Our grandmothers mixed bread by the time-honored method we give here. We prefer this method, as we think it gives top results, but there are several modern methods that are quick and easy and well worth using when time is short.

CoolRise Rapidmix way was developed by Robin Hood Flour and Fleischmann Yeast. This method allows you to mix without dissolving the yeast, and eliminates the second rising.

Mix the undissolved yeast with the flour, sugar, and salt. Combine the milk or water with the shortening and heat until very warm. Gradually add dry ingredients, beating well. Use enough flour to make a stiff dough. After kneading the dough, allow it to rise for 20 minutes, while you are cleaning up and greasing the bread pans. The dough is then shaped into loaves, placed in the pans, covered, and allowed to rise in the refrigerator for from 2 to 48 hours, until convenient to bake. This is a very useful method if you do not have time to make bread from start to finish, or if you wish to serve bread hot from the oven to your guests. For detailed instructions write to Fleischmann for their recipe book "Bake-It-Easy Yeast Book." The address is Standard Brands, Inc., 625 Madison Avenue, New York, New York 10022. This book is full of many good recipes for all kinds of breads.

Pillsbury has a recipe book called "Fast'n Easy Yeast Baking," which may be had by writing to the Pillsbury Co., Minneapolis, Minnesota 55402. Their method mixes yeast into the other dry ingredients, without dissolving it first, and relies on thorough beating with an electric mixer to reduce the kneading time to 1 minute or to eliminate it entirely. This bread requires two risings; the time saved is in the mixing and short kneading.

Another time-saving method was developed in the Betty Crocker Kitchens. This bread requires buttermilk and both yeast and baking powder. Since this dough needs only one rising and bakes in 30 minutes, more time is saved. To our minds it hasn't the flavor of our time-honored method. Write to Betty Crocker Kitchens, P.O. Box 1113, Minneapolis, Minnesota 55440, for their recipe book, "Breads to Bake with Yeast."

Time-Honored Mixing Method For Yeast Breads

First read the recipe through from beginning to end. Assemble all ingredients on the counter before starting and remember they must be at room temperature. Use all-purpose, pre-sifted and unbleached flour.

1   Place the shortening, salt, sugar, or other sweetening in a large bowl. Stir in the hot liquid. Allow to cool slightly, until a few drops placed on the inside of the wrist feel neither hot nor cold. Dissolve yeast and a bit of sugar in ¼ cup of warm water, tested for temperature in the same way. Let it stand until it froths, then add to the mixture. If it doesn't froth, either the yeast is too old or you have forgotten the sugar.

2   Add 2 cups of flour in the beginning, beating vigorously, either by hand for 300 strokes using a wooden paddle or spoon, or with an

electric mixer for 1 minute at low speed, then 2 minutes at medium speed, scraping the sides of the bowl frequently. This will develop the gluten, enabling the dough to rise well. Stir in by hand enough of the remaining flour to make the dough roll away from the sides of the bowl. If you are using mixed flours, begin with two cups of white flour, then add the dark flours, and finally as much more white as needed to make the dough the proper consistency.

3 Sprinkle the bread board with flour, turn the dough onto the board, lightly flouring both your hands and the top of the dough, and knead. As you work add only enough flour so that the dough is no longer sticky. Remember that rye flour is naturally sticky, and so is dough containing honey, so be careful not to add too much flour when kneading them.

To knead, press the palms of your hands against the front of the mass of dough, and push away from you. Fold the back of the dough

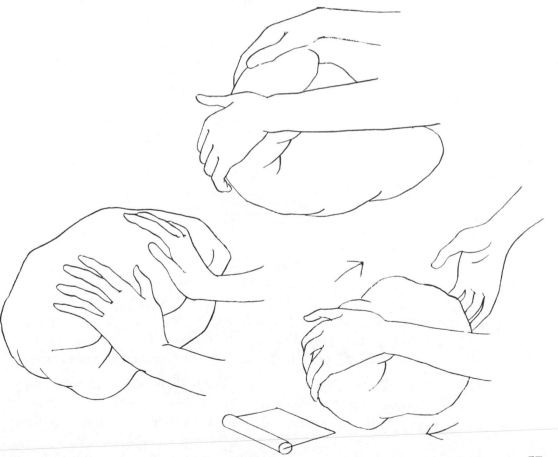

toward the front, give it a quarter turn, and again roll it away from you with the palms of your hands. Repeat until the dough appears satiny and feels bouncy, and blisters show at the surface, about 10 minutes. Don't skimp on kneading, for it will make the bread fine-textured and light.

4   Oil the mixing bowl, form the dough into a ball, and place smooth side down, then turn over to coat both sides with the oil. Cover the bowl with a piece of plastic wrap or wax paper so that a crust will not form on top of the dough, top with a dish towel for warmth, and put in a warm and draft-free place to rise. A gas oven with a pilot light is a good place, or an electric oven that has had the heat turned on for a few seconds to remove the chill, but not long enough for the element to turn red. Let rise until double in bulk. Dark flours will not rise as high as white flour, nor as quickly, but if indentations made by pressing two fingers into the dough remain, it has risen sufficiently. Do not hurry the rising process. Slow rising gives better flavor.

5   When the dough is light, turn onto a lightly floured board and knead again for about 5 to 10 minutes, using as little flour as possible. Pull apart or cut with a knife into as many loaves as the recipe calls for. If allowed to rest for 10 to 15 minutes at this point, the dough will be easier to form into shapely loaves, and the bread will be lighter.

6   Shaping the loaves: if the dough is soft, shape into an oblong, pressing it down with your fingers to remove bubbles. Make an indentation lengthwise along the center with the side of your hand,

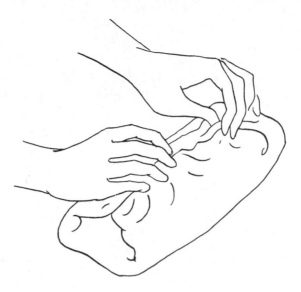

bring the two sides to the center and pinch together to seal. Tuck the ends in and pinch in the same way. Turn sealed side down in a well-greased pan, press with your fingers to fill the pan and remove bubbles, leaving the center higher and making a well-rounded loaf. A stiffer dough is very easy to form into a loaf by pressing into an oblong and then patting the sides with the palms of your hands till it forms a well-shaped loaf, rounded on top. Place in a well-greased loaf pan.

For a round free-form loaf, make a ball and flatten slightly, and bake either in a pie plate or on a well-greased cookie sheet that has been generously sprinkled with cornmeal. For a long loaf, roll the dough back and forth with the palms of your hands to the desired shape and place on a cookie sheet.

Cover the loaf with greased plastic wrap and let it rise again until the dough has either risen an inch above the top of the pan in the center or in the case of free-form loaves, until they have nearly doubled in bulk.

7   Glaze if you wish (see "Glazes" in "Tips, Terms, and Ingredients"). Bake for 10 minutes in a preheated oven set at 375°, then reduce heat to 325° and bake for 25 to 45 minutes, or as specified in the recipe. If the loaf begins to brown during the first 10 minutes, your oven is too hot. If after the first 10 minutes it browns too rapidly, cover with an aluminum foil tent. The bread is done when it is nicely brown and starting to pull away from the sides of the pans. Remove from the oven and turn out of the pan immediately. If the sides of the loaf are very soft, or not sufficiently brown, or if the loaf does not sound hollow when thumped on the bottom with your fingers, put it back in the pan and return to the oven for another 5 minutes. If in doubt, stick a thin, sharp knife into the loaf from the bottom, well into the center. If it comes out clean the bread is done. Cool loaves on their sides on a wire rack. Do not cover with a cloth unless you want a very soft crust. If you have not already glazed the loaf, spread a little soft butter over the top just as it comes from the oven.

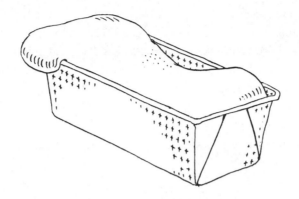

5 **What Went Wrong?**

YEAST BREADS

CRUST IS DARK AND HARD, AND INTERIOR OF LOAF HEAVY. The oven was too hot.

CRUST IS PALE AND INSIDE DRY. The oven was too cool, so that the bread cooked too slowly.

THE GRAIN OF THE BREAD IS COARSE. Oven temperature too low or too long a rising period is responsible for this. The loaf will also be coarse, with low volume, if not sufficiently kneaded.

THE LOAF IS SPLIT AT THE TOP. Either the oven was too hot, or it has hot spots. See "Ovens" under "Tips, Terms, and Ingredients."

THE BREAD ROSE UNEVENLY, ONE SIDE HIGHER THAN THE OTHER, DURING BAKING. This is also caused by hot spots in your oven. Place loaves on the diagonal to allow better heat circulation.

THE TOP OF THE LOAF IS SUFFICIENTLY BROWN AND THE LOAF DONE, BUT SIDES AND BOTTOM ARE STILL VERY PALE AND SOFT. This is due to unseasoned, shiny pans or Teflon pans (see "Utensils," also under "Tips, Terms, and Ingredients"). Remove the bread from the pans, place on a cookie sheet, and return to the oven for 5 minutes or until brown enough. If the top begins to brown too much, cover with an aluminum foil tent. Baking the loaves on the bottom shelf will help prevent this problem.

THE TOP OF THE LOAF SLUMPED AND CREASED. Either the proportion of liquids to drys was too great, or the dough was not kneaded long enough.

THE BREAD IS SOGGY. Either too much liquid was used, or the loaves were not properly cooled. They should be removed from the pans immediately, cooled uncovered on wire racks so that the steam may escape. However, bread in molds may be difficult to turn out. Wait 5 to 10 minutes and then turn out and cool on racks.

THERE IS EXCESSIVE VOLUME, AND THE BREAD IS FULL OF HOLES. Dough that has risen a little too long will have excessive volume and be full of holes. Dough that has risen *much* too long, on the other hand, will have low volume and be coarse and dry.

THE LOAVES ARE HARD AND HEAVY. The dough did not rise long enough. It should be allowed to rise until double in bulk and indentations remain after pressing two fingers into the dough.

THE LOAF IS MISSHAPEN. The dough rose too high. Dough too soft or too stiff could also be responsible.

THE DOUGH SPREAD OVER THE TOP OF THE PAN. Either the pan was too full or the dough had risen too much. With a kneaded dough, fill the pans two-thirds full and let rise an inch above the top of the pan in the center.

THE UNKNEADED BATTER BREAD ROSE BEAUTIFULLY, BUT FELL WHILE BAKING. The dough was allowed to rise too high. Never fill pans more than half full nor allow the dough to rise higher than the top of the pan. If it has risen higher than that, punch down and allow to rise again.

LOAVES BAKED ON A COOKIE SHEET SPREAD TOO MUCH. The dough was too soft. Next time knead in enough flour to make a stiffer dough.

QUICK BREADS

THE BREAD IS DRY, HEAVY, AND FULL OF HOLES AND TUN-NELS. Too vigorous mixing will cause this. Quick breads should have a minimum amount of mixing, quickly done with a light hand.

THE LOAF FELL IN THE MIDDLE DURING BAKING. Your pans were too full. Pans for quick breads should be only half full.

THE LOAF SPLIT ON TOP. All quick breads do this. The bread will split more neatly and evenly if you make a lengthwise cut in the dough with a wet knife about half an inch deep, just before putting the loaf into the oven.

RECIPES

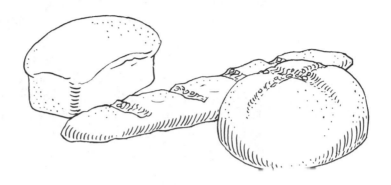

6 Kneaded Yeast Breads

Basic Yeast Bread

2 to 4 TBS. shortening (butter,
   margarine, or cooking oil)
2 to 3 TBS. sweetening (sugar,
   honey, or maple syrup)*
2 cups hot liquid (milk, buttermilk, vegetable or meat
   broth, potato or rice water)

2 tsp. salt
   (for white bread†)
1 TBS. active dry yeast
   (for white bread†)
   dissolved in
¼ cup warm water with
½ tsp. sugar
6 cups flour, approximately

* You can use ¼ to ½ cup of molasses in place of the sweetening.
†If you want to make whole grain bread instead of white, use 2 TBS.
active dry yeast instead of 1. For whole grain or cereal bread, use 1
TBS. salt.

    Place shortening, sweetening, and salt in a large bowl. Add the
hot liquid. Dissolve the yeast in water which feels neither hot nor

cold when a drop is placed on the inside of the wrist. Let stand until it froths and increases in volume, then add to the mixture. Add 2 cups of white flour, beating with an electric mixer set at low speed for 1 minute. Increase speed to medium and beat for 2 minutes. If you do not use a mixer, beat by hand for 300 strokes. If your recipe calls for dark grain flour, add that next, stirring it in by hand. Then add sufficient additional white flour to make the dough roll away from the bowl. Turn out onto a floured bread board and knead for about 10 minutes, until the dough is satiny and elastic, and has a dimpled appearance. Oil the bowl, form the dough into a ball and place in the bowl, turning to coat both sides with the oil. Cover with plastic wrap, add a towel for warmth, and let rise in a warm, draft-free place until double in bulk. Punch down and knead again for 10 minutes. Divide the dough into two balls, cover with plastic and let rest for 15 minutes, while you are cleaning up. Shape the balls into loaves and place in greased bread pans. Cover again with plastic wrap and let rise until the dough is about an inch above the top of the pans in the center. If you plan to use a glaze, brush it on now. Bake on the center shelf in a preheated oven, according to the recipe you are using. The bread is done when the loaf sounds hollow when tapped on the bottom with your fingers. Remove from pans immediately and cool on a wire rack.

Yield: 2 average loaves.

TIPS

FLOURS. When using dark and light flours, first use 2 cups of white flour and beat well with an electric mixer to develop the gluten, then stir in all the dark flour by hand, followed by as much of the remaining white as necessary to make the dough roll away from the bowl.

For whole grain breads, a mixture of whole grain and white flours will give a lighter loaf.

Herbs and spices may be added. See the sections on "Herbs" and "Spices" in "Tips, Terms, and Ingredients" for amounts.

SUGAR. For better flavor, use light brown sugar instead of granulated white for white breads. Use dark brown sugar or molasses for whole grain breads.

EGGS. Warm eggs will give greater volume and therefore lighter bread.

LIQUIDS. Water will give a crustier bread than milk, but the bread will dry out more quickly.

It is not necessary to scald pasteurized milk, but unpasteurized milk must be scalded to kill enzymes which prevent the yeast from working.

YEAST. If you are doubling a recipe calling for 2 tablespoons of yeast, use 3 tablespoons, not 4. In halving a recipe calling for 1 tablespoon of yeast, use whole amount.

All ingredients must be at room temperature, except liquids, which should be warm enough so that a drop on the inside of the wrist feels neither hot nor cold.

High Rise White Bread

Plain but good, and loved by children. It makes good toast.

¼ cup butter or margarine
1 TBS. salt
2 TBS. light brown sugar
1 cup warm milk
¾ cup warm water

1 TBS. active dry yeast,
    dissolved in
¼ cup warm water with
1 tsp. sugar
6 cups unbleached
    white flour

Place butter, salt, and sugar in a large bowl. Stir in the milk and water. Let the dissolved yeast stand until it froths and increases in volume, then add to the mixture. Add 2 cups flour, beating with an electric mixer at low speed for 1 minute; increase speed to medium and beat for 2 minutes. Or beat vigorously by hand for 300 strokes. Stir in enough additional flour by hand to make the dough roll away from the bowl. Turn out on a floured board and knead for about 10 minutes, until the dough is satiny and elastic, and has a dimpled appearance. Oil the bowl, form the dough into a ball and place in the bowl, turning to coat both sides with oil. Cover with plastic wrap and a towel, place in a warm, draft-free place, and let rise until double in bulk, about 2 hours. Punch down and knead again for about 5 minutes. Divide in two, cover with the plastic and let rest for 15 minutes, then shape into two loaves. Place in greased bread pans, cover, and let rise until the dough is an inch above the top of the pans. Brush with milk and bake in a hot oven, 400° for 15 minutes, then reduce heat to 350° and bake 35 to 45 minutes. Turn out of pans immediately and cool on a wire rack.

Yield: 2 average loaves.

Cloud 9 Bread
(High-Protein White with Soya)

A delicate, light bread, truly delicious. Very nutritious for children.

¼ *cup powdered milk*
4 *TBS. butter or margarine*
1 *TBS. salt*
⅓ *cup honey*
2 *cups hot milk*
2 *eggs, beaten*

1 *heaping TBS. active*
   dry yeast dissolved in
½ *cup warm water with*
1 *tsp. sugar*
1 *cup soya flour*
6 *to 7 cups unbleached*
   white flour

Place in a bowl the powdered milk, butter, salt, and honey. Pour the hot milk over them and stir. When the mixture is warm, add the beaten eggs and dissolved and foaming yeast. With an electric mixer beat in 2 cups of white flour at low speed for 1 minute, increase the speed to medium and beat for 2 minutes, scraping down the sides of the bowl frequently, or beat vigorously by hand for 300 strokes. Stir in the soya flour by hand, then enough additional white flour to make the dough roll away from the bowl. Turn onto a lightly floured bread board and knead for 10 minutes, or until the dough is satiny and shows bubbles just below the surface, using only enough flour to keep the dough from sticking. Form into a ball and place in an oiled bowl.

70

Turn to coat both sides evenly, then cover with plastic wrap and a towel and allow to rise in a warm and draft-free place until double in bulk. Punch down and knead again for 10 minutes. Divide the dough into two balls, cover with plastic, and let rest while you clean up. Then shape into loaves and place in greased pans. Cover and let rise until nearly double in bulk. Bake at 350° for 10 minutes, reduce heat to 325° and bake about 35 minutes longer. This bread browns rapidly and should be covered with a foil tent after about 20 minutes. When done, turn out of pans immediately and cool on wire racks.

Yield: 2 average loaves.

Midge's White Bread

This bread has a good, mellow flavor and makes delicious sandwich bread. We are indebted to Midge Wyman for this delightful recipe.

1 TBS. *butter or margarine*	1 TBS. *active dry yeast*
2 *tsp. salt*	*dissolved in*
2 TBS. *molasses or honey*	¼ *cup warm water with*
¾ *cup powdered milk*	½ *tsp. sugar*
2 *cups hot water*	5 *to 6 cups unbleached*
	white flour
	½ *cup soya flour*

Place butter, salt, honey or molasses, and the dry milk in a large bowl. Stir in the hot water. Allow to cool until the mixture feels neither hot nor cold when dropped on the inside of the wrist, and add the dissolved and frothing yeast. Add 2 cups of white flour, and beat for 1 minute with an electric mixer set at low speed. Increase speed to medium and beat for 2 more minutes. Stir in the soya flour by hand and add enough additional white flour to make the dough roll away from the bowl. Turn onto a floured board and knead until the dough is satiny and elastic and bubbles show below the surface. Form into a ball and place in an oiled bowl, turning the ball to coat both sides. Cover with plastic wrap and a towel, and let rise in a warm and draft-free place. This is a slow-rising bread of low volume. When the dough has doubled in bulk, knead again for about 10 minutes. Cover with the plastic and let rest for about 15 minutes. Shape into two loaves and place in greased pans. Cover with greased plastic and a towel and let rise again until the dough rises just above the top of the pans. Bake at 350° for 40 minutes, or until the loaves sound hollow when thumped. Remove from pans and cool on wire racks.

Yield: 2 average loaves.

Raisin Cinnamon Bread

A really good tea bread, equally good toasted for breakfast.

2 cups hot buttermilk	2 TBS. active dry yeast
3 TBS. light brown sugar	dissolved in
3 TBS. butter or margarine	¼ cup warm water with
2 tsp. salt	½ tsp. sugar
2 tsp. cinnamon	4½ to 5 cups unbleached
	white flour
	1½ cups raisins

If the raisins are hard and dry, refresh them by placing in a saucepan and covering with cold water. Bring to a boil, remove from heat and let stand for 5 minutes. Drain well, spread on a paper towel, and pat dry.

Mix the hot buttermilk, sugar, butter, and salt in a large bowl. Let the yeast mixture stand until it froths and add to the first mixture. Sift the cinnamon into 2 cups of flour and beat into the buttermilk mixture with an electric mixer set at low speed for 1 minute, then increase speed to medium and beat for 2 minutes, or beat vigorously by hand for 300 strokes. Stir in lightly floured raisins and enough of the remaining flour to make the dough roll away from the sides of the bowl. Turn out on a floured board and knead for 10 minutes, or until the dough feels bouncy and shows air bubbles under the surface. Oil a bowl and place the ball of dough in it, turning to coat both sides.

Cover with plastic wrap and a towel, put in a warm, draft-free place, and let rise until double in bulk, about 1¼ hours. Punch down and knead again for about 10 minutes. Cover with plastic and let rest for 10 minutes. Divide in two and shape into loaves. Place in greased pans and cover with greased plastic wrap and a towel. Let rise again until nearly double in bulk, about 1 hour. Brush with milk and bake in a preheated 375° oven for 10 minutes, then reduce heat to 350° and bake for 35 to 40 minutes more, or until the loaf sounds hollow when thumped on the bottom. Turn out of the pans immediately and cool on a wire rack.

Yield: 2 average loaves.

VARIATION

Add the grated rind and juice of 1 large orange.

White Buttermilk Bread

A light and delicious bread, which makes excellent toast.

2 cups hot buttermilk
2 TBS. light brown sugar
3 TBS. butter or margarine
2 tsp. salt

1 heaping TBS. active dry
   yeast dissolved in
¼ cup warm water with
½ tsp. sugar
4½ to 5 cups unbleached
   white flour

Mix the hot buttermilk, sugar, butter, and salt in a large bowl. Let the yeast mixture stand until it froths and add to the first mixture. Beat in 2 cups of flour, using an electric mixer set at low speed for 1 minute, then increase speed to medium and beat for 2 minutes. Or beat by hand vigorously for 300 strokes. Add enough of the remaining flour to make the dough roll away from the sides of the bowl. Turn out on a floured board and knead for 10 minutes, or until the dough feels bouncy and shows air bubbles under the surface. Grease a bowl and place the ball of dough in it, turning to coat both sides. Cover with plastic wrap and a towel, put in a warm, draft-free place, and let rise until double in bulk, about 1 hour. Punch down and knead again for about 10 minutes. Cover with plastic and let rest for 10 minutes. Divide in two and shape into loaves. Place in greased pans, cover with greased plastic wrap and a towel, and let rise again until nearly double in bulk, about three-quarters of an hour. Bake in a preheated 375° oven 10 minutes, reduce heat to 350° and bake for 35 to 40 minutes more, or until the loaf sounds hollow when thumped on the bottom. Remove from pans and cool on a wire rack.

Yield: 2 average loaves.

VARIATION

Substitute 1 to 3 cups of either whole wheat, rye, or graham flour for an equal amount of white, and use dark brown sugar instead of light brown. Spices or herbs may be added if desired. See "Tips, Terms, and Ingredients" for amounts.

White Wheat Germ Bread

A very good and flavorful bread, which also makes good toast.

2 cups hot water
3 TBS. sesame oil*
3 TBS. light brown sugar
1½ tsp. salt

1 TBS. active dry yeast
   dissolved in
¼ cup warm water with
½ tsp. sugar
½ cup wheat germ, raw
5 to 6 cups unbleached
   white flour

Sesame oil gives a nutty flavor to the bread, but plain cooking oil may be substituted if you wish.

In a large bowl mix together the water, oil, sugar, and salt. Add the dissolved and foaming yeast. With an electric mixer beat in 2 cups of white flour at low speed for 1 minute. Increase the speed to medium and beat for 2 minutes, scraping down the sides of the bowl frequently. Or beat vigorously by hand for 300 strokes. Stir in the wheat germ by hand, followed by enough white flour to make the dough roll away from the sides of the bowl. Turn onto a lightly floured board and knead for 10 minutes, or until the dough is elastic and shows bubbles under the surface. Use only enough flour to prevent the dough from sticking. Form into a ball and place in an oiled bowl. Turn to coat both sides evenly and cover with plastic wrap and a towel. Allow to rise in a warm, draft-free place until double in bulk. Punch down and knead again for 10 minutes. Divide the dough into two balls, cover with plastic, and let rest while you clean up. Then shape into loaves and put in two moderate-sized pans, approximately 7 by 4 by 2 inches. Cover with greased plastic wrap and let rise until nearly double in bulk. Bake at 375° for 10 minutes, then reduce heat to 325° for 35 to 40 minutes. Turn out onto a wire rack immediately to cool.

Yield: 1 large or 2 medium loaves.

French Bread

The unique flavor of traditional French bread is the result of several slow risings and of baking in a French professional baker's oven, which is brick-lined or tile-lined and sprays steam over the loaves during the first minutes of baking. Our simplified home version of a long, complicated process results in bread of excellent flavor and texture that is well worth the time and effort it takes. It will be even better if you adapt your oven to approximate the French; instructions for doing this are given under "Ovens" in "Tips, Terms, and Ingredients." French bread is at its best eaten fresh, for it dries out quickly. If you have some a day or two old, sprinkle it with water and reheat to refresh (see "Reheating," also in "Tips, Terms, and Ingredients").

According to French law, their bread contains only flour, water, salt, and yeast. We have added a half teaspoon of sugar to make the yeast work better.

2 cups warm water
2 tsp. salt
6 cups unbleached white
  flour, or enough to
  make a soft dough

1 TBS. yeast dissolved in
¼ cup warm water with
½ tsp. sugar

Place the water and salt in a large bowl. Add the dissolved, foaming yeast. With an electric mixer set at low, beat in 2 cups of flour for 1 minute. Increase speed to medium and beat for 2 minutes, scraping down the sides of the bowl frequently. Or beat vigorously by hand for 300 strokes. Stir in by hand enough flour to make the dough roll away from the sides of the bowl. It will be soft and sticky. Knead in the bowl with a wooden paddle until the dough has enough body to knead on a board. Cover the board with a floured pastry cloth, tucking the edge of the cloth under the edge of the board nearest you, to keep it from slipping during kneading. The cloth is essential, for the dough will still be very sticky. Knead until the dough is satiny and elastic and shows air bubbles under the surface. The dough must rise slowly at room temperature until it is three and a half times greater in volume, about 3 hours. Since the recipe makes 4 cups of unrisen dough, it will equal 14 cups when it has risen sufficiently. To gauge this accurately, pour 14 cups of water into the bowl you plan to use and mark the water level, or measure the remaining distance from the water to the top of the bowl. Empty and dry the bowl, and oil it. Form the dough into a ball and place in the bowl, turning to coat both sides. Cover with plastic wrap and a towel, set on a folded bath towel for additional warmth, and let rise until it reaches the 14-cup mark. If the rising is hurried, there will be loss of flavor.

Turn out onto the floured cloth and knead again for several minutes. Don't be rough, but get out the bubbles. Allow to rise a second time to less than three times in volume. To gauge this rising, again measure the water level, this time using 11 cups of water. This rising will be much faster, approximately an hour. Turn out on the floured cloth and knead for 2 minutes, pricking out the bubbles with a toothpick. Flatten the dough gently into a rectangle and cut into three equal parts. Fold each over, cover with greased plastic wrap, and let rest for 10 minutes. Then form each piece into a long loaf with the palms of your hands, fold over lightly lengthwise, and pinch to seal. Roll the loaf back and forth with your hands until the loaves are nearly as long as your cookie sheet, again pricking out any bubbles.

Place the loaves on a large greased cookie sheet that has been liberally sprinkled with cornmeal, preferably white. Cover with greased plastic and let rise again until nearly three times in bulk. This will probably take less than an hour.

Preheat oven to 400° and place a shallow pan of boiling water on the floor of the oven. Just before putting the loaves in, slash them with three diagonal slashes, using a very sharp knife or a razor blade. Brush with cold water. Spray the loaves with cold water while baking, using a clean plant mister. Bake until light brown and crusty, 25 to 35 minutes. Remove from cookie sheet and place on wire racks to cool.

Yield: 3 loaves.

Kimani's Safari Bread

This bread evokes wonderful memories of East African safaris. We would leave camp at dawn to view game and come back ravenous around eleven or twelve o'clock. Kimani, the assistant guide and a gifted cook, always placed the breakfast table under the shade of the biggest tree. We fell upon the food, consuming plate after plate of Kimani's satisfying, filling toast. How good it tasted! Each safari began with a stock of bakery bread and not until it was gone did Kimani start baking. It was cause for great rejoicing when a hyena came into camp one night and made off with the remaining commercial bread.

Kimani baked four loaves at a time, in a metal camp oven just large enough to hold the loaves, and he covered it with hot coals to bake. We give two versions of this bread here, as well as his original recipe. We are most grateful to Kimani Kuria for allowing us to use it.

ORIGINAL RECIPE	TRANSLATED INTO AMERICAN MEASUREMENTS
2 kg. white flour	*17 cups unbleached white flour*
1 tsp. salt	*1¼ tsp. salt*
½ tsp. sugar	*⅝ tsp. sugar*
1 tsp. yeast	*1¼ tsp. yeast*
1½ pints water	*1⅞ pints water*

Mix together and knead half an hour. Let rise in tins until it puffs out and bake in a tin oven at 500°. Also you can make brown bread as well. Makes 4 loaves.

LUCY'S VERSION

One of our testers, Lucy G. Raup, who is an experienced camp cook and the author of a successful cookbook on the subject, kept as close to the original as possible, but halved the recipe. Because of the differences in flour and altitude, she increased the amount of salt and yeast. She considers this a good camp bread, so firm that it packs easily without crushing and cuts well with any old knife. And it will keep hunger at bay for many hours!

1 ½ tsp. active dry yeast,	8 ½ cups unbleached
dissolved in	white flour
1 ⅞ cups warm water with	2 tsp. salt
½ tsp. sugar	

Mrs. Raup followed Kimani's directions, but confesses that she didn't knead for half an hour! This is a very slow-rising bread. She baked it in her kitchen stove at 500° for approximately half an hour.

SAFARI AT HOME VERSION

This is a lighter and less dense version we have adapted for home use. It is a good sandwich bread and delicious toasted. All versions have a unique flavor. Freeze the extra loaf, as this bread dries out quickly, since it has no shortening.

2 cups warm water	5 cups unbleached
1 tsp. sugar	white flour
1 TBS. active dry yeast	2 tsp. salt

Pour the water into a large bowl with the sugar. Sprinkle the yeast on the water and stir in. When it has dissolved, beat in, with the electric mixer set at low speed, 2 cups of flour and the salt; beat for 1 minute. Increase speed to medium and beat for 2 minutes, scraping down the side of the bowl frequently. Or beat by hand for 300 strokes.

Stir in enough additional flour by hand to make a stiff dough. Turn onto a floured board and knead for 15 minutes or more. Cover with plastic wrap and a towel and let rise slowly at room temperature. Knead again for 10 minutes and shape into 2 loaves. Place in greased pans and cover. Let rise until the center of the dough is an inch above the sides of the pans. Bake in a 400° oven for 10 minutes. Reduce heat to 350° and bake 35 to 40 minutes more. The bread is done when it sounds hollow when rapped on the bottom of the loaf. Remove from pans and cool on wire racks.

Yield: 2 loaves.

Graham Cracker Bread

This unlikely sounding bread is perfectly delicious and children love it. It is a good sandwich bread.

2 cups hot milk
4 TBS. butter or margarine
2 tsp. salt
¼ cup honey
3 to 4 cups unbleached
    white flour

2 TBS. active dry yeast
    dissolved in
¼ cup warm water with
½ tsp. sugar
2 cups whole wheat flour
1 cup crushed Honey
    Graham crackers

Pour the milk into a large bowl and add the butter, salt, and honey. Add the dissolved, foaming yeast and stir. With an electric mixer set at low, beat in 2 cups of white flour for 1 minute. Increase speed to medium, beat for 2 minutes, scraping down the sides of the bowl frequently. By hand stir in the whole wheat flour and then the graham cracker crumbs. Add enough white flour to make a stiff dough. Turn onto a floured board and knead for 10 minutes, until the dough is satiny and elastic and air bubbles show under the surface. Cover with plastic wrap and a towel and let rise until double in bulk. Knead again for 10 minutes, divide into two balls, cover with the plastic, and let rest while you clean up. Form into loaves, place in greased pans, and cover. Let rise until the center of the dough is one inch from the top of the pans. Bake at 350° for 10 minutes, reduce heat to 325°, and bake for 35 to 45 minutes. Since this bread browns fast, watch it carefully. You will probably need to cover it with aluminum foil. Turn out of pan when done. Cool on a wire rack.

Yield: 2 average loaves.

VARIATION

This is also very good made with Wheatsels instead of the graham crackers. Wheatsels is a cereal that may be purchased from Walnut Acres, Penns Creek, Pennsylvania 17862.

Gluten Protein Toasting Bread

A high-protein, low-calorie bread which makes delicious toast.

2¼ cups hot water
1 TBS. salt
1 TBS. white vinegar
1¼ to 1½ cups unbleached
    white flour
1 cup whole wheat flour

3 cups gluten flour
½ cup soya flour
2 TBS. active dry yeast
    dissolved in
⅓ cup warm water with
½ tsp. sugar

Pour the water into a large bowl and add the salt and vinegar. Add the dissolved, foaming yeast and with an electric mixer set at low speed, beat in 1 cup of white flour for 1 minute. Increase the speed to medium and beat for 3 minutes more. Thoroughly mix together the whole wheat, gluten, and soya flours and stir vigorously by hand. Add sufficient white flour to make the dough roll away from the bowl. The dough will be sticky. Knead for 10 minutes, place in an oiled bowl, and turn to coat both sides. Cover with plastic wrap and a towel and let rise in a warm, draft-free place for 50 to 60 minutes. Punch down and knead again for 10 minutes. Divide into two balls, cover with plastic, and let rest for 20 minutes. Form the dough into two loaves and place in 8½ by 4½ by 2½ inch greased loaf pans. Cover with oiled plastic and a towel and let rise again until the dough is an inch above the pan in the center. Glaze with white of egg beaten with 1 tablespoon of water, and bake for 10 minutes at 375°. Reduce heat to 350° and bake for about 30 to 40 minutes, or until the loaf sounds hollow when tapped on the bottom. Turn out of pans immediately and cool on wire racks.

Yield: 2 medium loaves.

Helen's Health Bread

A delicate and slightly sweet whole grain bread, which is also delicious toasted. We are grateful to Helen Coolidge for allowing us to use this excellent recipe.

3 cups boiling water
1 cup dry milk
3 TBS. shortening
1 TBS. salt
2 cups quick rolled oats
⅔ cup maple molasses*

1 TBS. active dry yeast
   dissolved in
¼ cup warm water with
½ tsp. sugar
4 to 5 cups unbleached
   white flour
2 cups whole wheat flour
⅓ cup toasted wheat germ

Mix first 6 ingredients in a large bread bowl and let cool until a drop on the inside of your wrist feels neither hot nor cold. Stir in the dissolved yeast. Beat in 2 cups of white flour, add the whole wheat flour and wheat germ, beating vigorously. Add enough of the remaining white flour to make the dough roll away from the bowl. Turn out onto a floured bread board and knead for 10 minutes. Place the dough in an oiled bowl, turning the dough over to coat both sides. Cover with plastic wrap and a towel and let rise in a warm place until double in bulk. Knead again for 10 minutes. Let the dough rest for 10 minutes, then shape into three loaves and place in greased pans. Cover and let rise until double in bulk. Place in a cold oven, immediately turning it on to 400°. Bake for 15 minutes, reduce heat to 350°, and bake for another 30 minutes. Turn out of pans immediately and cool loaves on their sides on a wire rack.

Yield: 3 average loaves.

*Maple molasses is the last run of maple sap, and it is dark, thick, and tangy. If you are unable to find it in health food stores, it may be obtained from Mrs. Basil E. Coolidge, Petersham, Massachusetts 01366.

Whole and Cracked Wheat Bread

An excellent and filling bread which makes a very fine meal with soup and cheese.

1 cup cracked wheat	2 TBS. active dry yeast
2 cups hot water or stock	dissolved in
6 TBS. honey	½ cup warm water with
2 tsp. salt	1 tsp. sugar
4 TBS. oil or butter	3 to 4 cups unbleached
	white flour
	½ cup soya flour
	2 cups whole wheat flour

Place the cracked wheat, hot water, honey, salt, and oil into a large bowl. Add the dissolved, foaming yeast. With an electric mixer set at low speed, beat in 2 cups of white flour for 1 minute. Increase speed to medium and continue to beat for 2 minutes more. By hand stir in the soya flour and then the whole wheat flour. Add enough of the remaining white flour to make the dough roll away from the bowl. Turn onto a floured board and knead for 10 minutes, until the dough is smooth and elastic and shows blisters under the surface. Form the dough into a ball and place in an oiled bowl, turning to coat both sides with the oil. Cover with plastic wrap and a towel and let rise in a warm, draft-free place until double in bulk. Knead again for 10 minutes, divide the dough into two parts, cover with plastic, and let rest while you clean up. Shape into loaves and place in greased pans. Cover and let rise until it has again doubled in bulk. Bake at 375° for 10 minutes, then reduce the heat to 350° and bake for about 20

82

minutes or until the loaf sounds hollow when rapped on the bottom. Remove from pans and cool on wire racks.

Yield: 2 average loaves.

Whole Wheat Rice Bread

A moist and hearty bread which is also good toasted.

2 cups hot milk
½ cup molasses
2 tsp. salt
2 TBS. butter or margarine
1 cup cooked brown rice
1 egg, beaten

2 TBS. active dry yeast,
   dissolved in
¼ cup warm water with
½ tsp. sugar
3 to 3½ cups unbleached
   white flour
½ cup soya flour
3 cups whole wheat flour

Place the milk, molasses, salt, butter, and rice in a large bowl. Add the egg, then the foaming yeast. With an electric mixer set at low speed, beat in 2 cups of white flour for 1 minute. Increase to medium speed and beat for 2 minutes. Stir in the soya flour by hand, then the whole wheat flour. Finally add enough additional white flour to make the dough roll away from the bowl. Turn onto a floured board and knead for 10 minutes, until the dough is elastic and satiny and air bubbles appear under the surface. Form the dough into a ball and place in an oiled bowl, then turn so that both sides of the ball are coated with oil. Cover with plastic wrap and a towel and let rise in a warm, draft-free place until double in bulk. Punch down and knead again for 10 minutes, then divide dough into two parts. Cover with the plastic and let rest while you clean up. Form into two balls and place each in a greased 9-inch pie pan. Cover with greased plastic and a towel and let rise until double in bulk. Bake at 375° for 10 minutes, then at 325° for 25 to 30 minutes or until the loaf sounds hollow when thumped on the bottom. Butter the crust immediately on removing from the oven. Remove from pans and cool on wire racks.

Yield: 2 average loaves.

Uncle Ben's Seasoned Long Grain and Wild Rice makes an excellent substitute for brown rice.

Whole Wheat and Rye Bread (CoolRise Method)

If you lack the time to complete the whole bread-making process, you will find this excellent bread very convenient. It may also be made in the usual way.

1 cup hot milk
1 cup hot water
¼ cup oil
½ cup molasses
1 TBS. salt
¼ cup yellow cornmeal

2 TBS. active dry yeast
   dissolved in
¼ cup warm water with
½ tsp. sugar
4 cups unbleached
   white flour
1 cup whole wheat flour
1 cup rye flour

In a large bowl stir together the hot milk and water, oil, molasses, and salt. Let the dissolved yeast stand until foamy and add to the liquid mixture. Add the cornmeal and 2 cups of white flour and beat with an electric beater at low speed for 1 minute. Increase the speed to medium and beat for 2 minutes. Mix the whole wheat and rye flour together and stir into mixture by hand, adding enough white flour— about 2 cups—to make the dough roll away from the sides of the bowl. Turn on to a lightly floured board and knead for 10 minutes. Divide into two balls, cover with plastic and a towel, and let rise for 20 minutes in a warm, draft-free place. Shape into two loaves, place in greased pans, brush lightly with oil, and cover loosely with waxed paper and then with plastic wrap. Place in the upper part of the refrigerator for from 3 to 24 hours, according to when it is convenient for you to bake. Remove from the refrigerator, uncover, and let stand at room temperature for 15 minutes, while the oven is preheating.

Bake on the shelf just below the middle of your oven, at 400° for 30 to 35 minutes. Remove from pans and cool on a wire rack.

Yield: 2 average loaves.

Orange Light Rye Bread

A delicate and delicious bread, of good volume.

2 cups hot milk	1 TBS. active dry yeast
3 TBS. maple syrup	dissolved in
3 TBS. butter or margarine	¼ cup warm water with
2 tsp. salt	½ tsp. sugar
grated rind and juice of	5¾ cups unbleached
1 orange	white flour
	1 cup rye flour

Place the milk, maple syrup, butter, salt, orange rind, and juice in a large bowl. Add the dissolved yeast. With an electric mixer set at low speed, beat in 2 cups of white flour for 1 minute. Increase the speed to medium and beat for 2 minutes. Stir in the rye flour by hand, and enough of the remaining white flour to make the dough roll away from the sides of the bowl. Turn onto a floured board and knead until the dough is elastic and shows bubbles just under the surface, about 10 minutes. Form into a ball, place in an oiled bowl, turning to coat both sides. Cover with plastic and a towel and let rise until double in bulk. Knead again for 10 minutes. Divide into two balls, cover with plastic, and let rest while you are cleaning up. Shape into loaves, place in greased pans, cover, and let rise until nearly double in bulk. Bake at 375° for 10 minutes, then reduce heat to 325° and continue to bake for 25 to 30 minutes. When done, turn out of pans immediately and cool on a wire rack.

Yield: 2 loaves.

This is a very delicate bread. For a more robust rye, use 2 cups of rye flour and 4¾ cups of white, and if you wish, a little more orange rind and juice.

Another excellent variation, Orange Rye Tea Loaf, may be found under "Festive Breads."

Cumin Through the Rye

A gently spiced rye bread.

2 *cups boiling water*	½ *tsp. cumin seed, crushed*
¼ *cup quick oatmeal*	1½ *TBS. active dry yeast*
¼ *cup molasses*	*dissolved in*
¼ *cup butter or margarine*	¼ *cup warm water with*
⅓ *cup dark brown sugar*	½ *tsp. sugar*
1 *TBS. salt*	3 *to* 3½ *cups unbleached*
1 *TBS. orange rind*	*white flour*
2 *tsp. ground coriander*	3 *cups rye flour*

Combine in a large bowl the water, oatmeal, molasses, butter, sugar, salt, rind, and spices. Dissolve the yeast and let stand until it froths. Add to the mixture in the bowl. With an electric mixer beat in 2 cups of white flour at low speed for 1 minute. Increase speed to medium and beat for 2 minutes, scraping down the sides of the bowl frequently. Or beat vigorously by hand for 300 strokes. Stir in the rye flour by hand, followed by sufficient white flour to make the dough roll away from the bowl. Turn onto a lightly floured bread board and knead for 10 minutes, or until the dough is satiny and shows air bubbles at the surface, using only enough flour to keep the dough from sticking. Form into a ball and place in an oiled bowl. Turn to coat both sides evenly; cover with plastic wrap and a towel and allow to rise in a warm, draft-free place until double in bulk. Again turn onto a floured board and knead for 10 minutes. Divide the dough into two balls, cover with the plastic, and let rest while you clean up. Then form dough into round or long loaves and place on a cookie sheet or greased pie pans that have been generously dusted with cornmeal. Cover with greased plastic wrap and a towel and let rise until nearly double in bulk. Bake at 350° for 35 to 45 minutes. About 5 minutes before the bread is done, brush with white of an egg beaten into 1 tablespoon of water and return to the oven. This will give the bread an attractive shiny crust. Remove from pans and cool on wire racks.

Yield: 2 loaves.

VARIATION

Substitute 2 teaspoons of fennel seed and 4 teaspoons of dill seed for the cumin and coriander. This makes a spicier loaf.

Black Peasant Bread

If you use only one recipe in this book, it should be this one.

2 cups hot water	2 TBS. active dry yeast
2 TBS. grated bitter chocolate	dissolved in
3 TBS. oil	¼ cup warm water with
3 TBS. caramel	½ tsp. sugar
1 TBS. salt	2½ cups unbleached
3 TBS. molasses	white flour
¼ to ¾ tsp. cumin seed, crushed	1½ cups whole wheat flour
	2 cups dark rye flour
	⅓ cup cornmeal
	⅓ cup bran

In a large bowl mix together the hot water, chocolate, oil, caramel, salt, molasses, and cumin seed. (The instructions for making caramel can be found in "Tips, Terms, and Ingredients.") Add the dissolved and foaming yeast. With an electric mixer set at low speed, beat in 2 cups of white flour for 1 minute. Increase speed to medium and beat for 2 minutes. Mix the whole wheat, rye, cornmeal, and bran together thoroughly and stir in by hand. The dough should be rather stiff. If necessary, add a little more white flour. Turn onto a floured board and knead for 15 minutes. Don't skimp on the time, for this is a heavy dough and needs more kneading to produce a reasonably light loaf. Place in an oiled bowl, turning to coat both sides. Cover with plastic wrap and a towel and let rise in a warm, draft-free place until double in bulk, about an hour. Knead again, this time for 10 minutes. Divide into two balls and place in 8-inch pie plates that have been well greased and generously dusted with corn-meal. Cover with greased plastic and a towel and let rise again until double in bulk. Bake in a 375° oven for 30 to 35 minutes. Ten minutes before the loaves are done, brush with white of an egg beaten into 1 tablespoon of water and return to the oven for 10 minutes, or until the loaves sound hollow when thumped on the bottom. Remove from pans and cool on wire racks.

Yield: 2 loaves.

CoolRise Method

This recipe adapts well to the CoolRise method. If you do not have time to complete the bread-making process, proceed as above until after the first kneading. Divide the dough into two balls, place in pie plates, brush with melted butter or oil, and cover with plastic. Let rise at room temperature for 20 minutes. Add a loose covering of wax paper and place in the upper part of the refrigerator for 2 to 12 hours. When you are ready to bake, let stand at room temperature for 15 minutes while your oven is preheating. Bake as above.

Cheese Bread

A very good and versatile cocktail bread, delicate in flavor and light. It keeps well.

1 cup hot water	*1½ TBS. active dry yeast*
1 cup hot milk	*dissolved in*
2 TBS. butter or margarine	*⅓ cup warm water with*
1 TBS. light brown sugar	*½ tsp. sugar*
2 tsp. salt	*½ cup freshly grated*
	Romano or Parmesan cheese
	5½ cups unbleached
	white flour

Mix the water, milk, butter, sugar, and salt together in a large bowl. Add the dissolved and foaming yeast. Stir in the cheese and with an electric mixer set at low speed, beat in 2 cups of flour for 1 minute. Increase speed to medium and beat for 2 minutes, scraping down the sides of the bowl frequently. Or beat vigorously by hand for 300 strokes. Stir in by hand enough of the remaining flour to make the dough roll away from the sides of the bowl. Turn onto a floured board and knead for 10 minutes, or until the dough is satiny and elastic and air bubbles show under the surface. Form into a ball and place in an oiled bowl. Turn to coat both sides, cover with plastic wrap and a towel, and let rise in a warm, draft-free place until double in bulk. Knead again, cover with plastic, and let rest while you clean up. Form into two average-size loaves or four small ones (we make our own small pans 8 x 2½ x 2 inches from the heavy foil pans that frozen loaf cakes come in (see "Utensils," in "Tips, Terms, and Ingredients"). Bake at 400° for 10 minutes; reduce heat to 325° and bake for about 25 minutes. Cheese bread browns fast and should be carefully watched. If the loaves brown too rapidly, cover with an aluminum foil tent. The small loaves should not be baked as long as the large ones. Remove from pans and cool on wire racks.

Yield: 2 average loaves or 4 small ones.

VARIATIONS

Herbs and spices blend well with cheese. Amounts given in these variations are for the whole recipe, using dried herbs. Triple the amounts for fresh herbs. If you wish all loaves to be alike, add the herb or spice in the beginning. However, if you wish each loaf to be different, knead in the herb or spice during the second kneading, after you have divided the dough into loaves. You can use any of the following:

- 1 TBS. crushed dill seed

- 1 TBS. other herbs, rosemary, sage, mixed herbs, etc. (see the section on "Herbs" in "Tips, Terms, and Ingredients")

- 1 to 1½ tsp. freshly ground black pepper

- 1 TBS. Jane's Crazy Mixed-Up Salt (omit salt called for in recipe)

- ½ cup grated fresh onion

- 4 TBS. reconstituted dried onion

- 4 TBS. Lipton's Dehydrated Onion Soup Mix

Crazy Mixed-Up Bread

Crazy and mixed up it may be, but also very good. The five different grains give it an interesting flavor. Experiment with other grains and cereals.

2 cups hot milk
3 TBS. butter or margarine
½ cup molasses
2 tsp. salt
2 TBS. active dry yeast
   dissolved in
¼ cup warm water with
½ tsp. sugar

5 cups unbleached
   white flour
½ cup rye flour
½ cup whole wheat flour
½ cup yellow cornmeal
¼ cup buckwheat flour

Mix the milk, butter, molasses, and salt in a large bowl. Cool until a drop on the inside of the wrist feels neither hot nor cold. Dissolve the yeast and sugar in water and let stand until it froths. Add to the milk mixture. With an electric mixer set at low speed, beat in 2 cups of white flour for 1 minute. Increase speed to medium and beat for 2 more minutes, scraping sides of the bowl frequently. Or beat vigorously by hand for 300 strokes. Mix all the dark flours together thoroughly and stir in by hand. Then add enough additional white flour to make the dough roll away from the sides of the bowl. Turn onto a floured board and knead for 15 minutes, until the dough is satiny and elastic and air bubbles show just under the surface. This dough is rough and needs long kneading. Form into a ball and place in an oiled bowl. Turn the dough over in order to coat both sides, cover with plastic wrap and a towel, and let rise in a warm, draft-free place until double in bulk, about 1 hour. Punch down and knead again for 10 minutes. Cover and let rest while you clean up. Divide in half and form into two loaves. Cover with greased plastic wrap and a towel and let rise until just above sides of the pan, about 45 minutes. Bake in greased pans in a preheated 375° oven for 10 minutes. Reduce heat to 325° and bake for 20 to 30 minutes. This bread browns fast and should be watched. You will probably need to cover it with aluminum foil. Turn out of pans immediately after removing from the oven and brush with butter. Cool on wire racks.

Yield: 2 average loaves.

Roman Meal Bread

Robust and highly nutritious.

2 cups hot milk	1 TBS. active dry yeast
1½ cups Roman Meal cereal	dissolved in
⅓ cup honey or maple syrup	¼ cup warm water with
1 TBS. salt	1 tsp. sugar
4 TBS. oil	4 to 4½ cups unbleached
	white flour

In a large bowl mix together the milk, Roman Meal, honey, salt, and oil. Add the dissolved, foaming yeast. With an electric mixer set at low speed, beat in 2 cups of flour for 1 minute; increase speed to medium, and beat for 2 minutes. If mixed by hand, beat for 300 strokes. Scrape down the sides of the bowl frequently. Stir in by hand enough of the remaining flour to make the dough roll away from the sides of the bowl. Turn onto a floured board and knead for 10 minutes, or until the dough is satiny and elastic and air bubbles show under the surface. Form into a ball and place smooth side down in an oiled bowl. Turn to coat both sides, cover with plastic wrap and a towel, and let rise in a warm, draft-free place until double in bulk. Knead again, cover with plastic, and let rest while you clean up. Divide in two and form into loaves. Place in greased bread pans, cover with greased plastic wrap, and let rise just above the sides of the pan. This dough is fast rising, so watch it. Bake at 350° for 10 minutes, then reduce the heat to 300° and bake for 35 to 40 minutes more. The bread is done when it sounds hollow when thumped with your fingers on the bottom. Remove from pans and cool on wire racks.

Yield: 2 average loaves.

VARIATIONS

Substitute Wheatena for Roman Meal. You will need about 5 cups of flour.

Substitute granola for Roman Meal, using 1½ tablespoons yeast and 4½ to 5 cups of flour. This bread browns very quickly and should be covered partway through the baking process with aluminum foil. Makes one average and one small loaf.

Malt and Barley Bread

Moist, chewy, and soul-satisfying.

1½ cup Maltex cereal	*1½ TBS. active dry yeast*
½ cup molasses	*dissolved in*
3 TBS. butter or margarine	*¼ cup warm water with*
2 tsp. salt	*½ tsp. sugar*
1 cup hot milk	*4 to 5 cups unbleached*
1 cup hot water	*white flour*
	1 cup barley flour

Place the Maltex, molasses, butter, and salt in a large bowl. Add the milk and water. Cool until a drop placed on the inside of the wrist feels neither hot nor cold, then add the dissolved and foaming yeast mixture. With an electric mixer set at low speed, beat in 2 cups of white flour for 1 minute; increase the speed to medium and beat for 2 more minutes, scraping down the sides of the bowl frequently. Stir the barley flour in by hand and add enough white flour to make the dough roll away from the bowl. Turn onto a lightly floured bread board and knead until the dough is satiny and elastic and shows air bubbles under the surface—about 10 minutes. Form into a ball and place in an oiled bowl. Turn to coat both sides evenly, cover with plastic wrap and a towel, and allow to rise in a warm, draft-free place until double in bulk. Punch down and knead again for 10 minutes. Divide the dough into two balls, cover with the plastic, and let rest while you clean up. Form into two loaves and place in greased pans. Cover with greased plastic wrap and a towel and let rise until the dough is just above the pan. Bake at 375° for 10 minutes, then reduce the heat to 325° and bake for 20 to 30 minutes more. It will be done if the bread sounds hollow when rapped with your fingers on the bottom. For a shiny crust, glaze with the white of an egg beaten into 1 tablespoon of water, 5 minutes before removing the bread from the oven. Remove from pans and cool on a wire rack.

Yield: 2 average loaves.

Cornmeal Mush Bread

A delicate and economical bread, and a good way to use up leftover cornmeal mush or Indian pudding.

1 cup cooked cornmeal mush	1 TBS. active dry yeast
2 cups very hot water	dissolved in
2 tsp. salt	¼ cup warm water with
½ cup molasses	½ tsp. sugar
2 TBS. soft white shortening	6½ to 7½ cups unbleached
	white flour

Place the cornmeal mush and 1 cup of hot water in a blender and blend until smooth. In a large bowl mix together the mush, the rest of the water, salt, molasses, and shortening. Let the dissolved yeast stand until it froths and add to the mixture. Beat in 2 cups of flour, using an electric mixer set at low speed for 1 minute; increase to medium speed and beat for 2 minutes. Or beat vigorously by hand for 300 strokes. Add enough of the remaining flour to make the dough roll away from the sides of the bowl. It will be soft and sticky. Turn out onto a floured board and knead for 10 minutes, until the dough is satiny and elastic and air bubbles show under the surface. Clean and oil the bowl and place the ball of dough in it, turning to coat both sides. Cover with plastic wrap and a towel, put in a warm, draft-free place, and let rise until double in bulk, about an hour. Punch down and knead again for 10 minutes. Divide into two balls, cover with plastic, and allow to rest while you clean up. Shape into loaves and place in greased pans, covering with greased plastic wrap and a towel. Let rise again until the dough reaches the top of the pans. This will rise very fast the second time, taking about half an hour. Glaze with milk and bake in a 375° preheated oven for 10 minutes, then reduce the heat to 325° and bake for 35 to 40 minutes more. Turn out of pans and cool on wire racks.

Yield: 2 average loaves.

VARIATION

Substitute Indian pudding for the cornmeal mush and use ¼ cup of molasses, instead of ½ cup. This is a very fast-rising bread. The flavor is very delicate.

Oatmeal Bread

This excellent, delicately flavored bread is a good way to use up leftover breakfast cereal.

2 cups hot milk
1 cup cooked oatmeal
1 cup uncooked rolled oats
½ cup molasses or maple
  syrup
2 TBS. butter or margarine

1 TBS. salt
2 TBS. active dry yeast
  dissolved in
¼ cup warm water with
1 tsp. sugar
6 to 6½ cups unbleached
  white flour

Mix thoroughly in a large bowl the milk, cooked oatmeal, rolled oats, sweetening, butter, and salt. Add the dissolved and foaming yeast. With an electric mixer set at low speed, beat in 2 cups of flour for 1 minute, then increase speed to medium and beat for 2 minutes, scraping down the sides of the bowl frequently. Stir in by hand enough additional flour to make the dough roll away from the sides of the bowl. Turn onto a floured board and knead for 10 minutes, until the dough is satiny and elastic and shows air bubbles under the surface. Form the dough into a ball and place in an oiled bowl, turning to coat both sides with the oil. Cover with plastic wrap and a towel and let rise in a warm, draft-free place until double in bulk. Knead again for 10 minutes, divide the dough into two balls, and let rest, covered, while you clean up. Shape into loaves and place in greased bread pans. Cover and let rise until it has again doubled in bulk. Bake at 375° for 10 minutes, then reduce heat to 325° and bake for about 30 minutes. The bread will sound hollow when thumped on the bottom when it is done. Turn out of pans and cool on wire racks.

Yield: 2 average loaves.

Samp Cereal Bread

The samp cereal of our childhood was a very coarse hominy with large kernels, cooked on the back of the old coal stove for fourteen hours, and considered a great treat. Nostalgia prompted us to try this samp cereal, which is not true samp but made of half crushed wheat and half crushed corn. However it does make a delightful, crunchy bread.

2 cups boiling water	2 TBS. active dry yeast
¼ cup molasses	dissolved in
1 cup samp cereal*	¼ cup warm water with
2 tsp. salt	1 tsp. sugar
4 TBS. butter or margarine	1 egg, well beaten
	4½ to 5½ cups unbleached white flour

In a large bowl mix together the boiling water, molasses, samp cereal, salt, and butter. When mixture is warm, add the dissolved and foaming yeast and the egg. With an electric mixer set at low speed, beat in 2 cups of white flour for 1 minute. Increase speed to medium and beat for 2 minutes. Stir in enough flour by hand to make a reasonably stiff dough. Turn onto a floured board and knead for 10 minutes, until the dough is satiny and elastic and shows bubbles just under the surface. Form into a ball and place in an oiled bowl, turning to coat both sides evenly. Cover with plastic wrap and a towel and allow to rise in a warm, draft-free place until double in bulk. Punch down and knead again for 10 minutes. Divide dough into two balls and place in greased pie pans, flattening the loaves slightly. Cover with greased plastic wrap and a towel and let rise until nearly double in bulk. With a sharp knife slash the tops in a cross and bake in a 400° oven for 10 minutes. Reduce the heat to 350° and bake 20 to 30 minutes more. The bread is done when it sounds hollow when tapped with your fingers on the bottom. Remove from pans and cool on wire racks. This bread browns quickly, so watch carefully and cover with aluminum foil if necessary.

Yield: 2 loaves.

*Samp cereal may be obtained from The Vermont Craftsmen, Inc., Weston, Vermont 05161.

Sweet Potato Bread

This is a favorite of R.C.F.'s grandchildren.

1 cup hot milk
½ cup warm mashed sweet
   potato, fresh or canned
3 TBS. butter or margarine
½ cup molasses
2 tsp. salt
Rind and juice of 1 orange

½ tsp. cinnamon
2 TBS. active dry yeast
   dissolved in
¼ cup warm water with
½ tsp. sugar
5 cups unbleached
   white flour

Place the milk, sweet potato, butter, molasses, salt, orange rind and juice, and cinnamon, in a large bowl. Stir in the dissolved, foaming yeast. With an electric mixer set at low speed, beat in 2 cups of flour for 1 minute. Increase speed to medium and beat for 2 minutes, scraping down the sides frequently. Stir in by hand enough additional flour to make the dough roll away from the sides of the bowl. Turn onto a floured board and knead for 10 minutes, until the dough is shiny and elastic and bubbles appear under the surface. Form into a ball and place smooth side down in an oiled bowl, turning to coat both sides. Cover with plastic wrap and a towel and let rise until double in bulk. Punch down and knead again for 10 minutes. Divide dough into two parts, cover, and let rest while you clean up. Shape into loaves and place in greased pans or, if your dough is stiff enough, you may make round loaves and bake in greased 8-inch pie pans. Cover and let rise again until double. Bake at 375° for 10 minutes; reduce heat to 325° and bake for 35 to 40 minutes more. Turn out of pans immediately, brush with butter, and cool, uncovered, on wire racks.

Yield: 2 average loaves.

Squash Bread

A delicious, moist, fine-textured bread with a delicate and different flavor.

1½ cups warm milk
2 TBS. dark brown sugar
1 TBS. salt.
¾ cup warm cooked winter
   squash, well drained and
   mashed, fresh or frozen
3 TBS. soft butter or margarine
1 egg, well beaten

½ tsp. cinnamon
¼ tsp. cardamom, crushed
2 TBS. active dry yeast
   dissolved in
   cup warm water with
½ tsp. sugar
5 to 5½ cups unbleached
   white flour
½ cup soya flour

Place the milk, sugar, salt, squash, butter, egg, cinnamon, and cardamom in a large bowl. Stir in the dissolved, foaming yeast. With an electric mixer beat in 2 cups of white flour at low speed for 1 minute, then increase speed to medium and beat for 2 minutes. Stir in the soya flour by hand and add 2½ more cups of white flour. Knead in the bowl for a few minutes, adding just enough flour to handle, about ½ cup. Turn out on a floured board and knead for 10 minutes, using only enough flour to keep the dough from sticking. Form into a ball and place in an oiled bowl, turning to coat both sides evenly. Cover with plastic wrap and a towel and let rise in a warm, draft-free place until double in bulk. Punch down and knead again for 10 minutes. Divide in half, cover with plastic and let rest while you clean up. Shape into two loaves and place in greased pans. Cover and let rise until just above the edge of the pans. Glaze with egg yolk and water (see "Glazes" under "Tips, Terms, and Ingredients") and bake at 375° for 10 minutes, then reduce heat to 325° and bake for 25 to 30 minutes longer, or until the bread sounds hollow when thumped with your fingers. Since this bread browns rapidly, it should be watched carefully and covered with an aluminum foil tent if necessary. Turn onto wire racks to cool.

Yield: 2 average loaves.

Brown Rice Flour Bread

A moist, chewy bread with a different flavor.

2 cups hot milk	2 TBS. active dry yeast
½ cup honey	dissolved in
2 tsp. salt	¼ cup warm water with
4 TBS. butter or margarine	½ tsp. sugar
4 cups unbleached	1 cup brown rice flour
white flour	½ cup raw wheat germ
	¼ cup sesame seeds

Place the milk, honey, salt, and butter in a large bowl. Add the dissolved, foaming yeast. Add 2 cups of white flour and beat with an electric mixer at low speed for 1 minute. Increase speed to medium and beat for 2 minutes, scraping down the sides frequently. By hand, stir in the brown rice flour, wheat germ, and sesame seeds and mix well. Add enough additional flour to make the dough roll away from the bowl. Turn onto a floured board and knead for 10 minutes, until the dough is satiny and elastic and has a dimpled appearance. The dough will be sticky. Form into a ball, place in an oiled bowl, turning to coat both sides. Cover with plastic wrap and a towel and let rise until double in bulk. Punch down and knead again for 10 minutes. Divide the dough in half, cover with plastic, and let rest while you clean up. Shape into loaves and place in greased pans. Cover and let rise until nearly double in bulk. Brush with egg yolk and milk glaze. (See "Glazes" under "Tips, Terms, and Ingredients.") Bake at 350° for about 40 minutes. The bread is done when it sounds hollow when rapped on the bottom with your fingers. Turn out of pans immediately and cool on wire racks.

Yield: 2 average loaves.

7 Unkneaded or Batter Breads

If you are in a hurry or don't feel like fussing, try unkneaded batter bread. It will not be as fine-textured or as delicate as a kneaded bread and the crust will look rough, but it is a very useful variety of bread, not just because of the time saved, but because it is good in its own right.

In batter breads the gluten is developed by beating instead of kneading. Since the dough is not kneaded, it requires less flour and therefore the dough is less stable. These breads are easy to make; the only pitfall is that you must not allow them to rise above the pan in the second rising. Since they do not have the extra flour to support them, they will collapse in the middle while baking if they have risen too much.

Basic Batter Bread

2 to 4 TBS. shortening (butter,
   margarine, or cooking oil)
2 to 4 TBS. sweetening (sugar,
   honey, or maple syrup)*
2 tsp. or 1 TBS. salt†
2 cups hot liquid (water, milk,
   buttermilk, vegetable or meat
   broth, potato or rice water)

1 TBS. or 2 TBS. active
   dry yeast‡ dissolved in
¼ to ⅓ cup warm water with
½ tsp. sugar
5 to 5½ cups flour

*You can use ¼ to ½ cup molasses instead of sweetening.
†Use 2 tsp. salt for white bread, 1 TBS. for whole grain and cereal bread.
‡Use 1 TBS. active dry yeast for white bread, 2 TBS. for whole wheat bread.

     Place shortening, sweetening, and salt in a large bowl. Add the hot liquid. Dissolve the yeast in water which feels neither hot nor cold when a drop is placed on the inside of the wrist. Let stand until it froths and increases in volume, then add to the mixture. Add two cups of white flour and beat with an electric mixer for 1 minute at low speed; then increase the speed to medium and beat for 3 minutes more, scraping down the sides of the bowl frequently. If you do not use a mixer, beat hard by hand for 300 strokes. Stir in by hand enough additional flour so that the dough begins to roll away from the bowl. It will be very sticky and impossible to handle. Cover the bowl with plastic wrap and a towel and let rise in a warm, draft-free place until double in bulk. Stir down by beating vigorously by hand for 25 strokes. Spoon the batter into well-greased pans, filling them half full. Wet your fingers and smooth the surface of the batter, pushing it into the corners. Cover with plastic wrap. A watchful eye is needed to be sure that the second rising barely reaches the top of the pans. It generally takes half the time of the first rising. If, by chance, the batter rises too high in the pans and is too full of air bubbles, punch down and let rise a third time. This third rising will be even more rapid than the second, so stay near the kitchen! Bake in a 375° oven for 30 to 45 minutes, or according to the recipe. The bread is done when the loaf sounds hollow when rapped on the bottom. Turn out immediately and cool on wire racks.

Yield: 2 average loaves.

Batter breads, because of their soft consistency, lend themselves to round casseroles as well as simple fluted molds. They may be glazed with either egg or milk glazes (see "Glazes" in "Tips, Terms, and Ingredients"). Be sure to apply with a delicate hand, however, so the batter is undisturbed. If the browning is too rapid, cover with an aluminum foil tent. This is especially necessary if an egg glaze is used.

White Batter Bread

An excellent, light-textured bread of good flavor. Good for both sandwiches and toast. This recipe is an adaptation of one from an unknown inn in Michigan. We are indebted to Mrs. Dwight Perry for passing it on to us.

1 TBS. active dry yeast	*2 tsp. salt*
1¼ cups warm (not hot) water	*2 TBS. sugar*
2 TBS. soft white shortening	*3 cups unbleached white flour*

Sprinkle the yeast on warm water and stir until dissolved. Add shortening, salt, sugar, and 1½ cups of flour to the water and yeast. Beat with an electric mixer at medium speed for 2 minutes. Add the remaining 1½ cups of flour and blend with a spoon until smooth. Cover with plastic wrap and a towel and let rise in a warm place until double in bulk, about 1 hour. Stir down the batter by beating for 25 strokes. Spread the batter evenly in a greased 9 by 5 by 3 inch loaf pan. The batter will be somewhat sticky. Cover and let rise in a warm place until the batter is 1 inch from the top of the pan. Do not let it rise too much. Bake in a 375° oven about 45 to 50 minutes, until the bread is nicely brown and sounds hollow when tapped with your fingers. Remove from the pan and brush with butter. Cool on a wire rack. You may double the recipe if you wish two loaves. It freezes well, but do not butter the top of the loaf if you plan to freeze it.

Yield: 1 loaf.

VARIATION

When you have stirred down the batter after the first rising, divide it equally in three bowls. In the first mix in 4 tablespoons each of fresh chopped parsley and chopped chives or green onions; in the second bowl add 2 teaspoons of reconstituted instant minced onion or 2 tablespoons of finely chopped fresh onion; and to the third bowl add 1 teaspoon of crushed dill seed. Spoon into small pans, 5½ by 3 by 2 inches, and proceed as above. Bake for 25 to 30 minutes. If your pans are very shiny, bake on the bottom shelf for better browning. These little loaves are delicious with either soup or salad, or with cocktails.

Yield: 3 small loaves.

Egg Bread

A rich, light, and airy bread, reminiscent of the French brioche. Its fine texture resembles a kneaded bread rather than a batter bread. Increasing the sugar to one-half or three-quarters of a cup will produce a delicate tea loaf. An added charm is that it is quick and easy to make.

1 cup milk
¾ cup butter or margarine
2 tsp. salt
2 TBS. light brown sugar
4 eggs

2 TBS. active dry yeast
*   dissolved in*
½ cup warm water with
½ tsp. sugar
5½ cups unbleached
*   white flour*

Place milk and butter in a saucepan and warm until the butter melts. Add salt and sugar and pour into a large bowl. Beat the eggs well until light in color. Reserve 1 tablespoon for a glaze and stir the rest into the milk mixture. Add the dissolved, foaming yeast. With an electric mixer set at low, beat in 2 cups of flour for 1 minute. Increase speed to medium and continue beating for 3 minutes. Stir in by hand sufficient additional flour to make the batter begin to roll away from the bowl. Cover with plastic wrap and a towel and let rise in a warm, draft-free place until double in bulk. Punch down and beat for 25 strokes. Divide in two and place in well-greased bread pans or in one-quart casseroles. They should not be more than half full. Cover with greased plastic wrap and let rise until the dough just reaches the top of the pans. Just before putting loaves in the oven, glaze with the reserved egg mixed with 1 tablespoon of milk. Bake at 375° for about 40 minutes. The bread is done when it sounds hollow when rapped on the bottom. Watch carefully for overbrowning and use an aluminum foil tent if necessary. Remove from pans and cool on wire racks.

Yield: 2 loaves of good volume.

Oaten Bread

This bread isn't like the usual oatmeal bread, but is has a delectable flavor all its own. It's at its best when eaten soon after it comes out of the oven.

2 cups hot milk
2 TBS. butter or margarine
3 TBS. maple syrup
2 tsp. salt
½ cup wheat germ

2 TBS. active dry yeast
   dissolved in
¼ cup warm water with
½ tsp. sugar
3 to 3¼ cups unbleached
   white flour
¼ cup soya flour
2 cups oat flour*

In place of oat flour, you can use rolled oats that have been whirled in a blender until fine.

Mix the milk, butter, syrup, salt, and wheat germ together in a large bowl. Stir in the dissolved, foaming yeast. With an electric mixer set at low speed, beat in 2 cups of white flour for 1 minute, then increase speed to medium and beat for 3 minutes. By hand stir in the soya and oat flours. Add enough white flour to make a soft, sticky dough. Do not knead. Cover with plastic wrap and a towel and allow to rise in a warm, draft-free place until double in bulk. Stir down with 25 strokes. Spoon into two greased loaf pans or one round casserole, smoothing the dough with wet fingers. The pans should be only half full. Cover with greased plastic and a towel and let rise to the top of the pans, no higher. Bake at 375° for 10 minutes, reduce the heat to 325° and bake for another 30 to 35 minutes. The bread is done when it sounds hollow when tapped on the bottom. Remove immediately from the pans and cool on a wire rack.

Yield: 2 average loaves or 1 large round one. This is a low-volume bread.

Variation

Substitute 1 cup of whole wheat flour for 1 cup of white.

Herb and Cheese Bread

The cheese flavor with a whisper of herbs makes this an excellent bread to serve with salads.

1 cup hot milk	1 cup shredded sharp cheddar
1 cup hot water	cheese, tightly packed
2 tsp. salt	2 TBS. active dry yeast
¼ tsp. sage	dissolved in
½ tsp. marjoram	⅓ cup warm water with
½ tsp. thyme	½ tsp. sugar
	4 to 5 cups unbleached
	white flour

Place the hot milk and water, salt, herbs, and shredded cheese in a large bowl. When mixture is warm, add the dissolved and foaming yeast. With an electric mixer, beat in 2 cups of flour at low speed for 1 minute. Increase speed to medium and beat for 3 minutes, scraping down the sides of the bowl frequently. By hand stir in enough of the remaining flour to make the batter just roll away from the sides of the bowl. Place batter in a greased bowl, cover with plastic wrap and a towel, and let rise in a warm and draft-free place until double in bulk. Punch down and beat with 25 strokes. Spoon into two greased pans, filling them only half full. Cover with greased plastic wrap and let rise again until the batter just reaches the top of the pans. Brush with milk and bake at 375° for 10 minutes; then reduce heat to 350° and continue baking for about 50 minutes or until the bread sounds hollow when tapped on the bottom. Remove from pans and let cool on wire racks.

Yield: 2 average loaves.

Grandmother's Oatmeal Bread

This recipe is given as my grandmother wrote it. Today's measurements are in parentheses, added for easier mixing. This has long been a favorite in my family. We always ate it toasted for breakfast, drenched in butter.

3 pints boiling water (6 cups)
1 cup molasses
1 handful sugar (2 TBS.)
1 tsp. salt

1 yeast cake (1 TBS.
   active dry yeast)
1 rounded pint Old Fashioned
   Quaker Oats (2 rounded cups)
White flour (12½ cups
   approximately)

Mix together the water, molasses, sugar, and salt. When mixture is cool, add a yeast cake and the Quaker Oats. Add enough flour to make a stiff dough. Stir and let rise in bowl 3 or 4 hours. Put in pans and rise again until up (reaches top of pan), about 1 hour. (Bake 45 minutes at 375°.)

Yield: 4 loaves.

Variation on My Grandmother's Theme

This is a lighter bread than the original, with a crisp crust.

3 cups hot water	1 TBS. active dry yeast
1 well-rounded cup	dissolved in
Quaker Oats	¼ cup warm water with
½ cup molasses	½ tsp. sugar
2½ tsp. salt	5½ to 6 cups unbleached
3 TBS. butter or margarine	white flour

Mix water, Quaker Oats, molasses, salt, and butter in a large bowl. When a drop of this mixture feels neither hot nor cold when placed on the inside of the wrist, add the yeast which has been dissolved in warm water and allowed to stand until it froths. With an electric mixer set at low speed, beat in 2 cups of flour for 1 minute, then increase the speed to medium and beat for 3 minutes, scraping down the sides of the bowl frequently. Or beat by hand for 300 strokes. Do not knead. Place the dough in an oiled bowl, turning to coat both sides evenly. Cover with plastic wrap and a towel and let rise in a warm, draft-free place until double in bulk. Punch down and stir for 25 strokes. Divide into two parts and place in greased pans. Pour 2 tablespoons melted butter over the loaves, sprinkle with more Quaker Oats, and press gently into the dough. Cover with a towel and let rise until dough reaches the tops of the pans. Bake at 350° for about 50 minutes.

Yield: 2 loaves.

Add the juice and rind of 1 large orange. Measure the juice and reduce the amount of water by that amount.

Kasha Bread

A substantial, full-flavored crunchy bread.

2 cups hot milk
¾ cup raw Kasha
   (buckwheat groats)
2 tsp. salt
4 TBS. oil
2 TBS. dark brown sugar
2 to 2½ cups unbleached
   white flour

2 TBS. active dry yeast,
   dissolved in
¼ cup warm water with
½ tsp. sugar
1 cup buckwheat flour
1 cup whole wheat flour

Place the hot milk, Kasha, salt, oil, and brown sugar in a large bowl. Add the dissolved and foaming yeast. With an electric mixer, beat in 1½ cups of white flour at low speed for 1 minute. Increase speed to medium and beat for 3 minutes, scraping down the sides of the bowl frequently. By hand stir in the buckwheat and whole wheat flours and finally enough of the remaining white flour to make the batter roll away from the sides of the bowl. Batter will be sticky. Cover the bowl with plastic wrap and a towel and let rise until double in bulk. Stir down, beating with 25 strokes, and spoon into two greased pans, filling them only half full. Cover and let rise again just to the top of the pans. If batter breads rise too much they will fall in the middle while baking. Bake in 375° oven for 10 minutes, reduce heat to 325° and bake another 35 to 45 minutes, until the bread sounds hollow when tapped on the bottom. Turn out of pans immediately and cool uncovered on wire racks.

Yield: 2 loaves.

Shredded Wheat Bread

A very popular bread. It is moist and rather heavy, with a unique flavor. Try it toasted for breakfast, swimming in butter.

2 shredded wheat biscuits
2 cups boiling water
1 TBS. salt
½ cup molasses
3 TBS. butter or margarine

1½ TBS. active dry yeast
   dissolved in
¼ cup warm water with
½ tsp. sugar
5 to 5½ cups unbleached
   flour

Break shredded wheat into a large bowl and add boiling water, salt, molasses, and butter. When mixture is warm, add the dissolved yeast. Stir in the flour, beating vigorously. The dough should be sticky. Cover with plastic wrap and a towel and let rise in a warm, draft-free place until double in bulk. Punch down and stir, but do not knead. Divide the dough into two greased pans, handling gently. Let rise again until the dough reaches the top of the pans. Bake in 350° oven for 45 to 55 minutes, or until the bread sounds hollow when rapped on the bottom of the loaf. Turn immediately onto a wire rack, butter the top of the loaves, and let cool.

Yield: 1 large or 2 small loaves.

Cornmeal Bread

An open-textured bread with a real cornbread flavor, good for toast or sandwiches. It has been described by one 7-year-old as "the best bread in the whole world."

2 TBS. light brown sugar
1 TBS. (scant) salt
2 cups buttermilk
2 TBS. butter
2 eggs

2 TBS. active dry yeast
   dissolved in
⅓ cup warm water with
½ tsp. sugar
½ tsp. baking soda
4 to 4½ cups unbleached
   white flour
¾ cup yellow cornmeal

Place sugar and salt in a large bowl. Heat the buttermilk and butter together until the butter melts. Pour into the bowl and stir. Beat the eggs, slowly add a little of the hot milk mixture to the eggs, stirring constantly. Then gradually stir the eggs into the rest of the milk mixture. Dissolve the yeast and when foaming add to the milk and eggs. Add the soda to 2 cups of the white flour, mixing thoroughly to prevent streaky bread. With an electric mixer set at low speed, beat the flour into the milk for 1 minute. Increase the speed to medium and beat for 3 minutes. Or beat vigorously by hand for 300 strokes. By hand stir in the cornmeal and enough additional white flour to make the dough leave the side of the bowl. It will be very sticky. Do not knead. Cover with plastic wrap and a towel and place in a warm, draft-free place until double in bulk. This is a quick-rising dough and the first rising will take about 45 minutes. When it has risen double in bulk, punch down and beat hard for 25 strokes. Spoon into two greased loaf pans, smoothing the batter into the corners with wet fingers. Let rise until it reaches the top of the pans, no further or it will fall while baking. This will take 30 to 40 minutes. Bake at 375° for 10 minutes; reduce heat to 350° and bake for 30 to 40 minutes more. Watch for overbrowning and cover with an aluminum foil tent if necessary. The bread is done when it sounds hollow when tapped on the bottom. Remove from pans and cool on a wire rack.

Yield: 2 smaller-than-average loaves.

Rye and Injun Bread

Crusty, crunchy, and country-style.

½ cup bacon fat or white
  shortening
¼ cup maple molasses or syrup
2 tsp. salt
2 cups hot water

2 TBS. *active dry yeast*
  dissolved in
⅓ *cup warm water with*
½ *tsp. sugar*
2½ *to 3 cups unbleached*
  white flour
1 *cup yellow cornmeal*
2 *cups rye flour*

Place the bacon fat, maple molasses, and salt in a big bowl and add the hot water. Stir in the dissolved, foaming yeast. With an electric mixer set at low speed, beat in 2 cups of white flour for 1 minute. Increase speed to medium and beat for 3 minutes. Thoroughly combine the cornmeal and rye flours and stir in by hand. Add just enough additional white flour to make the batter roll away from the bowl. It will still be very sticky. Place in a lightly oiled bowl, cover with plastic wrap and a towel, and let rise in a warm, draft-free place until double in bulk. This will take about 50 minutes. Punch down and stir vigorously for 25 strokes. Spoon into two greased bread pans, cover with greased plastic wrap, and let rise again until the dough just reaches the top of the pan. It will take approximately 40 minutes. Bake in a 375° oven for about 40 minutes. It is done when the loaf sounds hollow when tapped on the bottom, and when a wooden toothpick inserted into the center comes out clean. Turn out onto a wire rack to cool.

Yield: 2 average loaves.

Lemon Whole Wheat Bread

The subtle lemon flavor contrasts wonderfully with the occasional bite of pepper. Lovely crunchy crust. It smells heavenly when toasting—and tastes the same!

2 cups milk
2 TBS. butter or margarine
¼ cup honey
2 tsp. salt
¾ tsp. freshly ground black pepper
grated rind of 1 lemon

2 TBS. active dry yeast dissolved in
⅓ cup warm water with
½ tsp. sugar
2 to 3 cups unbleached white flour
1 TBS. lemon juice
2 cups whole wheat flour

Heat the milk and butter together until the butter melts. In a large bowl place the honey, salt, pepper, and grated lemon rind, and add the milk mixture. Stir in the dissolved, foaming yeast. With an electric mixer set at low speed, beat in 1½ cups of white flour for 1 minute, increase speed to medium, and beat for 3 minutes more. Add the lemon juice and whole wheat flour, stirring in vigorously by hand. Add enough additional white flour to make the dough just begin to roll away from the sides of the bowl. Place in an oiled bowl, cover with plastic wrap and a towel, and allow to rise in a warm and draft-free place until double in bulk, about an hour. Punch down and beat hard for 25 strokes. Place part of the batter in a greased one-quart casserole and part in a bread pan, filling each half full, or if you prefer, use two bread pans. Cover with greased plastic wrap and allow to rise just to the top of the pans. Bake at 375° for 10 minutes, reduce heat to 350°, and bake for 30 to 40 minutes more, or until the bread sounds hollow when rapped on the bottom. Brush the tops with butter, remove from pans and cool on a wire rack.

Yield: 2 medium loaves or 1 large loaf.

8 Festive Yeast Breads

From time immemorial, bread has had religious significance. In pagan times it was an offering to the gods, in Christian times it symbolizes the body of Christ. No festival is complete without fancy breads. In the Ukraine they are an integral part of wedding ceremonies. In Sardinia the wedding breads are delicate beyond belief, resembling a lacy valentine more than a loaf of bread. All through Europe special breads are part of the Christmas and Easter celebrations.

Give a family meal a festive air by baking special breads: sweet dough, with spices, raisins, and nuts for Sunday breakfasts or for a coffee klatch; dark breads with spices for lunch or dinner, braided or molded into attractive shapes. For a fisherman's birthday, bake his favorite bread in a fish-shaped mold. For a child's birthday, bake a sweet bread in a three-dimensional lamb mold and tie a ribbon and some flowers around its neck. Stick balls of dough together to resemble a turtle. Even the most ordinary bread looks festive if it is baked in intriguing shapes, in a pretty mold or a braid. Experiment. You will find it great fun.

MOLDS

Season a new mold by placing it in a 350° oven until it loses some of its brilliance. Fluted molds, jelly molds of all designs, three-dimensional molds, casseroles, all make attractive loaves. Let bread

cool in the mold for 15 minutes for easier removal, then place on a wire rack. Breads may be decorated with a white glaze and a wreath of red and green candied cherries for Christmas, with sugar mints in the shapes of flowers and leaves for Easter.

BRAIDS AND OTHER SHAPES

Braids are easy to make, and they give a festive air to the simplest lunch of soup or salad. After the second kneading, divide the dough into three parts, roll between your palms into ropes, and starting in the middle, braid loosely to each end and then pinch the ends together. Make a two-story braid, placing a three-strand braid on top of a four-strand braid, tucking the ends of the top braid into the

116

bottom one to secure it. A small braid laid on top of an ordinary pan loaf transforms it into a party loaf. Glaze with egg or milk and the results will be very professional.

For Easter, divide the dough into two parts and twist *very* loosely, pinching the ends together to form a ring. Slip an uncooked, gaily colored Easter egg into each twist, let rise and bake, and there is your child's complete breakfast!

Make a Christmas tree by braiding five strands for the branches and three for the trunk.

Make a rolled and filled loaf. First roll out your dough into a rectangle, about 9 by 14 inches. Spread it with a fruit filling (see "Fillings" under "Tips, Terms, and Ingredients"), roll firmly along the short side, pinch the ends of the roll firmly, and place seam side down on a greased cookie sheet or bread pan. Let rise, and bake. Or roll along the long side, seal the ends together to form a circle, and with sharp scissors cut from the outside three-quarters of the way through to the inner edge, every 1½ inches. Pull cut pieces apart gently and bake on a cookie sheet.

If you aren't the type that likes to fool around with dough, bake any festive bread recipe in an ordinary loaf pan and give it a festive touch with an egg glaze and a topping of coarse sugar (we use Swedish pearl sugar, available at Scandinavian delicatessens, or crushed rock candy). Or sprinkle the loaf with seeds or nuts (see "Toppings," also under "Tips, Terms, and Ingredients").

If instead of a festive bread you would like to serve French bread, give it a different look by making a flute. Divide dough into three parts and roll into long thin loaves. Just before baking, slash with a very sharp knife on alternating sides, all the way down the

loaves. Or break off small pieces of dough and form them into rolls, with pointed ends. Join them together, overlapping the points at a slight angle, first on one side, then on the other, the length of the cookie sheet you will bake them on. It is attractive looking and instead of slicing the bread, each person breaks off a roll. These will bake faster than the conventional French loaf, so watch them carefully.

The recipes for festive breads given here are for all occasions; some are sweet, others not. They are all out of the ordinary.

Basic Sweet Dough

*The upper figures given for butter and sugar make a very rich
bread. For a plainer one use the lower figures.*

½ to 1 cup sweet butter
½ to 1 cup light brown sugar
2 well-beaten eggs
2 tsp. salt

2 TBS. active dry yeast
    dissolved in
¼ cup warm water with
1 tsp. sugar
1½ cups warm milk
6 to 7 cups unbleached
    white flour

Cream butter and sugar together and add the eggs and salt. Stir
the dissolved yeast into the warm milk and add to the first mixture.
Beat in the flour vigorously, adding enough to make a soft dough.
Turn onto a lightly floured board and knead until the dough is satiny
and elastic. Place in a greased bowl, turn to coat both sides evenly,
cover with plastic wrap and a towel, and let rise in a warm, draft-free
place until double in bulk. Punch down and knead for 3 minutes.
Cover with plastic and let rest while you clean up. For shaping festive
loaves, see the instructions at the beginning of this chapter. Recipes
for fillings, glazes, and toppings may be all found in the chapter
"Tips, Terms, and Ingredients." Bake at 350° for 30 to 35 minutes, or
according to the recipe. Sweet breads should be watched carefully for
overbrowning, and covered with aluminum foil if necessary.

Honey Bread

A sweet bread for a very special breakfast.

2 cups hot milk
½ cup butter or margarine
½ cup honey
2 tsp. salt

2 TBS. active dry yeast
    dissolved in
½ cup warm water with
1 tsp. sugar
2 eggs
6 cups unbleached
    white flour

Mix the milk, butter, honey, and salt together in a large bowl. Let cool until the mixture feels neither hot nor cold when dropped on the inside of the wrist. Add the dissolved and foaming yeast, beat in the eggs. With an electric mixer set at low speed, beat in 2 cups of flour for 1 minute, then increase the speed to medium and beat for 2 minutes, scraping the sides of the bowl frequently. Or beat by hand for 300 strokes. Stir in by hand enough of the remaining flour to make the dough roll away from the sides of the bowl. Dough will be soft. Turn onto a lightly floured board and knead for 10 minutes, or until the dough is satiny and elastic and air bubbles appear under the surface. Form into a ball and place in an oiled bowl, turning to coat both sides. Cover with plastic wrap and a towel and allow to rise in a warm, draft-free place until double in bulk. Punch down and knead again for 3 minutes. Cover with the plastic and let rest for 10 minutes. Shape into two large loaves, or into braids. Place in greased pans, or, for the braids, on a greased cookie sheet. Cover with greased plastic wrap and a towel and allow to rise to the top of the pans. If you are using a cookie sheet, let rise until double in bulk. Bake for 10 minutes at 400°, reduce heat to 350° and bake until nicely browned. If the bread browns too quickly, cover with aluminum foil. Glaze with an egg yolk beaten with 1 tablespoon of water and sprinkle with granulated, pearl, or cinnamon sugar for the last 5 minutes of baking. Remove from pans and cool on wire racks.

Yield: 2 loaves.

VARIATIONS

After the second kneading, roll into two oblongs, making them an inch narrower than the length of the loaf pan. Brush with melted butter and sprinkle generously with cinnamon sugar. Roll up into loaves and place in greased pans. Or instead of sprinkling with cinnamon sugar, spread with a thin layer of honey. Bake as above.

For a different-flavored dough, substitute maple molasses for the honey.

Sweet Mace Bread

We think this bread is outstandingly delicious, and so does everyone who has tasted it.

3 cups hot milk	2 TBS. active dry yeast
1½ cups sweet butter	dissolved in
2 tsp. salt	¼ cup warm water with
1 cup light brown sugar	½ tsp. sugar
8 cups unbleached	½ cup citron
white flour	2 tsp. mace
	¾ cup golden raisins

If the raisins are hard and dry, refresh them by placing in a saucepan and covering with cold water. Bring to a boil, remove from heat, and let stand for 5 minutes. Drain well, spread on a paper towel, and pat dry.

Heat the milk and butter together until the butter melts. Allow to cool until a drop placed on the inside of the wrist feels neither hot nor cold. Add the salt, sugar, and the dissolved, frothing yeast. Add 2 cups of flour and beat with an electric mixer for 1 minute at low speed. Increase speed to medium and beat for 2 minutes. Stir in 4 more cups of flour by hand. Next add the citron, mace, and raisins that have been dredged in ¼ cup of flour. Add enough additional flour to make the dough roll away from the bowl. Turn out onto a lightly floured board and knead gently for 10 minutes. Place in an oiled bowl, turning to coat both sides. Cover with plastic wrap, add a towel, and set the bowl in a pan of hot water. Let it rise for 2 to 3 hours, until nearly tripled in bulk. Punch down, and knead lightly for a few minutes. Let rest for 10 minutes, then form into two very large loaves or three smaller ones. For a very festive occasion, make three braids and bake on a greased cookie sheet. Cover with greased plastic wrap and the towel and allow to rise until it reaches the top of the pans, or until the braids have doubled in bulk. Glaze with the white of 1 egg beaten into 1 teaspoon of water. Sprinkle with pearl sugar or crushed rock candy and bake for 10 minutes at 375°, reduce the heat to 350° and bake for 30 to 35 minutes more. Watch carefully for browning and cover with aluminum foil if necessary. When done, remove from pans or cookie sheet and cool on wire racks.

Yield: 2 very large loaves, or 3 average ones, or 3 braids.

Sunday Bread

A rich, sweet bread for a special Sunday or birthday breakfast.

½ cup butter
1 cup hot milk
½ cup light brown sugar
¾ tsp. crushed cardamom seed
1 tsp. salt
1 egg, beaten
1 TBS. brandy (optional)

1 TBS. active dry yeast
    dissolved in
¼ cup water with
1 tsp. sugar
4 cups unbleached
    white flour
½ cup golden raisins

If the raisins are hard and dry, refresh them by placing in a saucepan and covering with cold water. Bring to a boil, remove from heat, and let stand for 5 minutes. Drain well, spread on a paper towel, and pat dry.

In a large bowl mix together butter, milk, sugar, cardamom, and salt. Then add the egg, brandy and dissolved, foaming yeast. Add 2 cups of flour and beat with an electric mixer for 1 minute at low speed. Increase speed to medium and beat for 2 minutes. Stir in the raisins. Add enough flour, stirring in by hand, to make the dough roll away from the bowl. Use as little as possible, for this should be a very light bread. Turn onto a lightly floured board and knead gently, until the dough is satiny and elastic, adding only enough flour to handle, not more than ¼ to ½ cup. Place in an oiled bowl, turn to coat both sides, cover with plastic wrap and a dish towel, and allow to rise until double in bulk. Knead again for several minutes. Shape into a ball, place on a greased pie plate, and flatten slightly. Cover with greased plastic and a towel and let rise again until nearly double in bulk, about 30 minutes. Bake in a 350° oven for 30 to 35 minutes. If bread browns too quickly, cap with aluminum foil. Remove from pie plate and cool on a wire rack. Glaze while still warm. This bread looks very attractive if baked in a bundt pan or in a fancy mold. In this case it should be allowed to cool for 10 minutes before turning out.

GLAZE

Stir together 1 cup sifted confectioners' sugar and 2 tablespoons milk or light cream. Beat well. Drizzle on hot bread. For Christmas, trim immediately with a wreath of sliced almonds and red candied cherries cut in half and put on cut side down. Green candied cherries may be cut into leaves.

Yield: 1 loaf.

Grandmother's Bread Cake

Bread cake was popular in our grandparents' time but is not to be found in any modern cookbook, which is a pity, for it is delicious. More cake than bread, it is a sweet dessert or coffee loaf. I found this recipe in my grandmother's handwriting, in her recipe notebook. It must be close to 100 years old. As was usual at that time, directions were not included, and we have provided them. I have found a similar one in an old cookbook which says that bread cake improves with keeping. We can't vouch for that, for it never lasts long enough in our families to find out.

SPONGE

2 cups scalded milk	*1½ TBS. active dry yeast*
2 tsp. salt	*dissolved in*
4½ cups unbleached	*¼ cup warm water with*
white flour	*½ tsp. sugar*

Allow the milk to cool until a drop placed on the inside of your wrist feels neither hot nor cold. Add the dissolved and foaming yeast, then the salt. With an electric mixer set at low speed, beat in 2 cups of flour for 1 minute. Increase speed to medium and beat for 2 minutes more. Stir in by hand the remaining 2½ cups of flour. Cover with plastic wrap and a towel, set in a warm and draft-free place, and let rise until light, about 2 hours. Beat down with 25 strokes and proceed with the following:

¾ *cup soft butter*	*1 tsp. nutmeg*
2 cups granulated sugar	*2 tsp. cinnamon*
4 eggs, separated	*½ tsp. allspice*
2 TBS. brandy	*1 scant tsp. baking soda*
1 cup unbleached	*1 cup raisins*
white flour	

If the raisins are hard and dry, refresh them by placing in a saucepan and covering with cold water. Bring to a boil, remove from heat, and let stand for 5 minutes. Drain well, spread on a paper towel, and pat dry.

Cream the butter and sugar, beating until light. With an electric mixer beat the egg yolks until they are thick and lemon-colored, add the brandy, and stir into the butter mixture. Combine this mixture with the sponge, beating vigorously by hand until it is well incorporated. Sift together the cup of flour, spices, and baking soda. Stir into the dough, mixing thoroughly. Add the raisins next. Beat the egg whites until dry and fold in gently. Cover with plastic wrap and a towel and let rise in the bowl until doubled in bulk, about 1 hour. Stir down and pour into greased pans, cover with plastic, and let rise for 20 minutes. This recipe will make 2 average loaves or 4 small ones, and it makes attractive gifts if baked in fancy molds. Bake in a 350° oven for 35 to 45 minutes, depending upon size of pan. Watch carefully for browning. You will need to cover the loaves with aluminum foil after about 15 minutes. Let cool in the pan for 5 minutes—longer if you have used a fancy mold—before turning out on the wire racks. Ice with white frosting while hot (see "Frostings" in "Tips, Terms, and Ingredients"), and decorate with candied fruit or with pearl sugar and chopped almonds.

Yield: 2 average loaves or 4 small ones.

Whole Wheat Mace Bread

This is a light, rich bread with an elusive flavor.

¾ cup butter or margarine
2 cups hot milk
½ cup dark brown sugar,
   packed
2 tsp. salt
½ tsp. mace
2 eggs, beaten

1½ TBS. active dry yeast
   dissolved in
¼ cup warm water with
½ tsp. sugar
2 cups unbleached
   white flour
4 cups whole wheat flour

Melt the butter in the hot milk, place in a large bowl with the sugar, salt, and mace. When the mixture feels neither hot nor cold when dropped on the inside of the wrist, add the beaten eggs and the dissolved and foaming yeast. With an electric mixer set at low, beat in the white flour for 1 minute. Increase speed to medium and beat for 2 minutes. Or beat vigorously by hand for 300 strokes. Stir in the whole wheat flour by hand. Add only enough extra white flour to make the dough possible to knead. The dough should be quite sticky, so add only enough to facilitate handling. Knead for 10 minutes, until the dough is satiny and elastic. Place in an oiled bowl, turning once so that both sides are coated. Cover with plastic wrap and a towel and let rise in a warm, draft-free place for about an hour. This is a light dough and rises quickly. Punch down and knead again. It may be baked in two bread pans, or made into one large braid (directions for making a braid can be found at the beginning of this chapter). Divide into the number of pieces you will need for either loaves or braid, cover with plastic, and let rest for about 10 minutes. Shape as desired, place in greased pans or on a cookie sheet, cover with greased plastic and a towel, and let rise again until nearly double in bulk, about 45 minutes. Just before baking, glaze with an egg yolk mixed with 1 tablespoon water and sprinkle with pearl sugar. Bake at 400° for 10 minutes, reduce heat to 350° and bake for 30 to 40 minutes more. Remove from pans and cool on wire racks.

Yield: 2 loaves or 1 large braid.

Substitute 1 cup of rye flour for the whole wheat and use 5 to 6 cups of white flour.

Orange Rye Tea Loaf

We served this light and fragrant bread at a wedding and it was a huge success. Slice thin, with crusts left on, and spread with butter.

2 cups hot milk	1 TBS. active dry yeast
3 TBS. maple syrup	dissolved in
½ cup light brown sugar	¼ cup warm water with
packed	½ tsp. sugar
2 tsp. salt	5 cups unbleached
3 TBS. butter or margarine	white flour
Rind and juice of 1 orange	1 cup rye flour
¼ to ½ tsp. crushed cardamom	1 cup golden raisins

If the raisins are hard and dry, refresh them by placing in a saucepan and covering with cold water. Bring to a boil, remove from heat, and let stand for 5 minutes. Drain well, spread on a paper towel, and pat dry.

Mix the milk, maple syrup, sugar, salt, butter, rind and juice, and cardamom in a large bowl. Add the dissolved and foaming yeast. With an electric mixer set at low speed, beat in 2 cups of white flour for 1 minute. Increase the speed to medium and beat for 2 minutes. Stir in the rye flour by hand. Flour the raisins lightly and add. Stir in enough of the remaining white flour to make the dough roll away from the sides of the bowl. Turn onto a floured board and knead for 10 minutes, or until the dough is satiny and elastic and shows air bubbles under the surface. Form into a ball, place in an oiled bowl, turning to coat both sides. Cover with plastic wrap and a towel and let rise until double in bulk. Knead again for 10 minutes. Divide in half if you are using regular bread pans, or in four parts if you plan to use the small foil pans 8½ by 2½ by 2¼ inches (see "Utensils" in "Tips, Terms, and Ingredients"). Cover with plastic wrap and let rest while you clean up. Shape into loaves, place in the greased pans, cover with greased plastic wrap and a towel, and let rise until nearly double in bulk. Bake at 350° for 30 to 40 minutes. When done, remove from pans and cool on a wire rack.

Yield: 2 average loaves or 4 small ones.

Thanksgiving Bread

Leftover filling for a Thanksgiving squash pie was the genesis of this delicious bread. It is fragrant, spicy, and different. Braid it for a welcome gift.

¾ cup mashed winter squash*
½ cup thick cream
⅓ cup granulated sugar
3 TBS. dark brown sugar
2 tsp. salt
2 large eggs, slightly beaten
¾ tsp. cinnamon
¾ tsp. nutmeg
½ tsp. ginger
¼ tsp. mace

3 TBS. butter or margarine
1 TBS. brandy
Juice of 1 orange
1 TBS. grated orange rind
½ cup milk
2 TBS. active dry yeast
   dissolved in
⅓ cup warm water with
½ tsp. sugar
4½ to 5 cups unbleached
   white flour

You can use ½ pkg. frozen, well-drained squash instead.

Reserve 1 tablespoon of beaten egg. Place all ingredients except yeast mixture and flour in a saucepan and heat very gently, until a drop placed on the inside of your wrist feels neither hot nor cold. Put in a large mixing bowl and add the dissolved and foaming yeast. With an electric mixer set at low, beat in 2 cups of flour for 1 minute; increase speed to medium and beat for 2 minutes. Stir in sufficient additional flour to make the dough roll away from the bowl. The dough should be soft. Turn onto a lightly floured board and knead for 10 minutes, until the dough is satiny and elastic. Place in an oiled bowl, turning to coat both sides. Cover with plastic wrap and add a towel for warmth. Let rise in a warm, draft-free place until very light, about 1¼ hours. Punch down and knead again for 10 minutes. Divide in two, cover with the plastic, and let rest for 15 minutes. Shape into loaves and place in greased pans, pricking any bubbles with a toothpick. Cover with greased plastic and a towel and let rise again until the dough is about 1 inch above the top of the pan in the center, about 1 hour. Add 1 tablespoon of water to the reserved egg and glaze the loaves. Bake in a 350° oven for approximately 35 minutes. Watch carefully for browning and if necessary, cover with aluminum foil. Bread is done if it sounds hollow when rapped on the bottom of the loaf with your fingers. Turn onto wire racks to cool.

Yield: 2 average loaves.

Limpa

Our variation of the Swedish Christmas bread is delicious and easy to make.

Juice of 2 oranges
Enough hot water added to the orange juice to make 2 cups
Rind of 2 oranges, grated
3 TBS. butter or margarine
3 TBS. dark brown sugar
2 tsp. salt
1 TBS. crushed anise seed
1 tsp. crushed cardamom seed

2 TBS. caramel*
1 TBS. active dry yeast dissolved in
¼ cup warm water with ½ tsp. sugar
3 to 4 cups unbleached white flour
3 cups rye flour

*For making caramel, refer to "Tips, Terms, and Ingredients."

In a large bowl mix together the water, orange juice, rind, butter, sugar, salt, anise, cardamom, and caramel. Add the dissolved, foaming yeast. With an electric mixer set at low speed, beat in 2 cups of white flour for 1 minute; increase speed to medium and beat for 2 minutes. Or beat in by hand with 300 strokes. Stir in the rye flour by hand and add enough additional white flour to make the dough roll away from the sides of the bowl. Turn onto a floured board and knead for 10 minutes. Form into a ball and place in an oiled bowl. Turn to coat both sides evenly and cover with plastic wrap and a towel. Allow to rise in a warm, draft-free place until it has doubled in bulk. Knead again for 10 minutes. Divide the dough in half, cover with plastic wrap, and let rest while you clean up. Then form into round or long loaves and place on a cookie sheet or pie pans that have been well greased and generously sprinkled with cornmeal. Cover with greased plastic wrap and a towel and let rise until nearly double in bulk. Bake at 375° for 10 minutes, reduce heat to 350° and bake for about 30 to 35 minutes more. Five minutes before the loaves are done, glaze with the white of an egg beaten with 1 tablespoon of water; return to the oven and bake until the bread sounds hollow when rapped on the bottom. Remove from cookie sheet and cool on wire racks.

Yield: 2 loaves.

Saffron Bread

A delicately flavored bread that rises spectacularly while baking. Its golden color makes it especially suitable for Easter.

2 cups hot milk
¾ cup butter
¾ cup light brown sugar
¼ tsp. powdered saffron
2 tsp. salt
2 eggs

2 TBS. active dry yeast
   dissolved in
¼ cup water with
½ tsp. sugar
7½ cups unbleached
   white flour
½ cup golden raisins

Heat milk and butter together until the butter melts. Place sugar, saffron, and salt in a large bowl and stir in the milk mixture. When warm, add the eggs which have been beaten until very light, and then the dissolved and foaming yeast. Then add 6 cups of flour, 2 cups at a time; after each addition, beat with an electric mixer set at low for 1 minute and then increase speed to medium and beat for 2 minutes more. If the raisins are dry, place in a saucepan and cover with cold water. Bring to a boil, remove from heat and let stand for 5 minutes. Drain on paper towels and fold into the dough. Stir in by hand enough additional flour to make the dough roll away from the bowl. The dough should be soft and sticky. Turn onto a well-floured board and knead for 10 minutes, until satiny and elastic. Place in an oiled bowl, turning to coat both sides. Cover with plastic wrap and a towel and let rise in a warm, draft-free place until double in bulk, about 1½ hours. Punch down and knead for 3 minutes. Divide in half and place in large, well-greased pans. This makes an especially attractive loaf if baked in a 1½-quart casserole. Let dough rise to the top of the pans. The second rising will be quicker. Glaze with a whole egg mixed with 1 tablespoon of water, and bake at 375° for 10 minutes; reduce heat to 350° and bake for about 35 minutes longer. The bread must be watched closely for overbrowning. When it is a pale gold, cover with an aluminum foil tent. The loaf is done when it sounds hollow when tapped on the bottom. Remove from pans and cool on a wire rack.

Yield: 2 large loaves.

Apple Bread

A delicate apple-flavored festive loaf, and a beautiful sight to behold when made into a glazed braid. This bread was much enjoyed at a family gathering—after one meal, not a crumb left!

½ cup butter or margarine
½ cup dark brown sugar
2 tsp. salt
2 cups hot milk
2 eggs, well beaten

2 TBS. active dry yeast
   dissolved in
¼ cup warm water with
½ tsp. sugar
1 cup finely grated
   unpeeled apples
7 cups unbleached
   white flour
½ tsp. cinnamon
½ tsp. allspice

In a large bowl place the butter, sugar, and salt, add the hot milk. Beat the eggs well and stir in a little of the milk mixture, then gradually add the eggs to the rest of the milk, beating vigorously. Add the dissolved, foaming yeast. Stir in the grated apples. With an electric mixer set at low speed, beat in 2 cups of flour, sifted with the spices, for 1 minute. Increase speed to medium and beat for 2 minutes. Add 1 more cup of flour and beat for another 2 minutes. Stir in by hand 4 cups of flour, adding 1 cup at a time, beating well after each addition, until the dough rolls away from the bowl. The dough will be soft. Turn onto a floured board and knead for 10 minutes. Place in an oiled bowl, turn to coat both sides, cover with plastic wrap and a towel, and let rise in a warm, draft-free place until double in bulk, about 1½ hours. Punch down and knead for 3 minutes. Divide into two balls, cover with plastic, and let rest for 10 minutes. Shape into loaves and place in greased pans. Cover with greased plastic wrap and let rise until light, about ¾ hour. Or divide into six equal parts, make two braids, and bake on cookie sheets. Just before putting in the oven, glaze with an egg yolk beaten with 1 tablespoon of water. Bake at 375° for 15 minutes, reduce heat to 350° and bake 35 to 40 minutes longer, until the bread sounds hollow when thumped. Watch for browning and cover with an aluminum foil tent when it begins to darken. Turn onto a wire rack to cool.

Yield: 2 large loaves or braids.

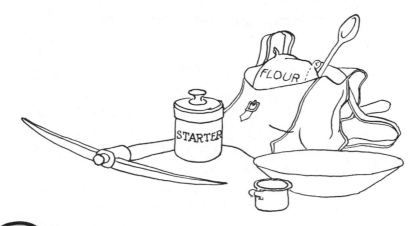

9 Sourdough Breads

Sourdough conjures up visions of cowboys and chuck wagons, prospectors and the Alaskan gold rush, and more recently, San Francisco restaurants. Actually, it is as old as bread and goes back 5000 years to the days of the Pharoahs, and perhaps further. The first sourdough in this country is said to have been brought here by Columbus.

Sourdough is a delectable, tangy, crusty bread of varying sourness, leavened with a starter containing wild yeast, which causes fermentation. The escaping gases make the dough rise in the same manner as commercial yeast. It may sound so complicated to make that you will feel discouraged before you start, but actually it is as easy as regular yeast bread, in some ways more so, and has the advantage of keeping well and freezing well. It is too delicious to miss, so do try it. And it will give you the reputation of being a fabulous breadmaker.

STARTERS

There are apocryphal tales of starters 100 years old, and certainly some starters are still living from Yukon days. They will last a long time if given proper care, and the flavor will improve with age. However, occasionally one will go bad, due to overheating or contamination, and must be thrown out.

HINTS ON CARE OF STARTER

Starter cannot stand as high a temperature as active dry yeast. Heat over 95° will kill it. It works fastest at 85°, but room temperature is good, since it gives the dough time to develop flavor. Starter becomes dormant when cold and so will keep well in the lower part of the refrigerator. In fact, it will keep indefinitely there if refreshed at least every two weeks. If you are not baking in that time, this is done by removing half your starter (give it away or freeze it) and replacing it with an equal amount of half flour and half water, well mixed. Leave it at room temperature until it bubbles, stirring once in a while. When you have taken out some of the starter to make a sponge (discussed in "Tips, Terms, and Ingredients" and later in this chapter under "Basic White Sourdough Bread"), replace it the next morning with the same amount from the sponge that has stood overnight, before the remaining ingredients have been added to it. Stir in thoroughly. In this way the starter will be maintained for many years.

Never store the starter in a metal container, for it will affect the flavor, and be sure to use a wooden spoon when mixing. The best container is a crock, but heavy glass or plastic will do, scalded before using. It should hold at least a quart. Do not fill it more than two-thirds full, leaving room for expansion, and do not cap tightly, particularly if you are using a glass container, for a well-working starter might shatter it. Label it, so that no one will consider it just an evil-smelling mess and throw it out.

If you like your bread decidedly sour, keep your starter at room temperature. In this case it must be used or refreshed every three or four days, less often if the weather is very hot. If it is kept refrigerated, it will make a delicately flavored bread.

When making dark breads, use white flour in the sponge, so that it stays pure for white bread, and add the dark flour with the remaining ingredients in the morning. Or keep a rye starter going.

134

If there is a crust or liquid standing on top, stir it in. This is normal and does not mean the starter has gone bad.

Freeze your starter when you go on vacation. Defrost at room temperature, and when it starts to bubble it is ready to use.

Every month or so, add a spoonful of sugar to your starter.

The number of different starters is legion. Experiment until you find the one you prefer. Each one gives a slightly different flavor to the bread. All starters are interchangeable in any recipe. There are commercial starters on the market. "Old Fashioned San Francisco Sourdough Starter," packed by the Gold Rush Sourdough Co., 1176 Market Street, San Francisco, California 94102, is a good one, and comes with recipes and directions for maintaining the starter. Crocks sold with starters obtained from mail order houses or from kitchen shops are apt to be much too small.

LUCY'S STARTER

Every sourdough cook has a favorite starter, and Lucy's is ours. We have used it in testing all the recipes in this book. Since it contains commercial yeast, it becomes ripe and ready for use more quickly than those with wild yeast. It has a delicate flavor, not aggressively sour. We are grateful to Lucy G. Raup for allowing us to use her starter recipe.

1 TBS. active dry yeast	*3 cups warm water*
1 tsp. sugar	*3 cups unbleached white flour*

Dissolve the yeast and sugar in the water. Add the flour, stirring until well mixed. Pour into a suitable nonmetal container (see "Hints on Care of Starter" in the previous section), and cover with cheesecloth. Keep at room temperature and away from drafts until it is bubbly and frothy, stirring every day. It will be ready for use in two or three days, depending on how warm the room is. When ready, cover with crock lid or plastic and store in the lower part of your refrigerator.

POPULAR STARTER

2 *cups warm water or*
  warm milk

2 *cups unbleached white flour*
1 *TBS. sugar*

If you use milk, which will make a stronger tasting starter, let it stand at room temperature for 24 hours, then mix in the flour and sugar. Put in a suitable container and cover with cheesecloth. If the weather is warm and dry, place outdoors or near an open window for a day to collect wild yeast. Then keep at room temperature until the mixture bubbles. This will take from two days to a week, depending upon the weather and upon how much wild yeast is in the air. When it is ready, cover with plastic and refrigerate. The flavor will improve as you use it.

RYE STARTER

Substitute rye flour for the white and proceed as in above recipe. Good for dark breads. Rye and milk make a very strongly flavored starter. It is not our favorite.

HINTS ON PREPARATION

As with all yeast breads, there are two methods of making sourdough breads, straight dough and sponge. While we advocate the former for yeast breads, we much prefer the sponge method for sourdough. The long rising time improves the flavor and, if started the night before, it enables you to have bread out of the oven by midmorning the next day. Also, a starter replenished from a sponge is of better consistency, livelier, and tastier. You will note that in making the dough, the addition of baking soda is optional in each recipe. The soda acts as a leavening agent and as such makes the bread a little lighter. On the other hand, it counteracts the sourness of the starter and makes the bread less tangy, with a milder sourdough flavor.

It is not necessary to add commercial yeast to sourdough bread, since 1 cup of starter will raise enough dough for two loaves, but the first morning rising will take 2 to 5 hours, depending on the warmth of the room and on the ingredients. Bread made this way is rather dense and chewy—and good. However, we prefer to add 1 tablespoon of active dry yeast, for the dough will be more dependable, the bread lighter, and the morning rising quicker. Try it both ways and decide which method you prefer. In making your own recipes, remember that a half cup of starter is equivalent to 1 tablespoon of active dry yeast or 1 cake of compressed yeast. You may also incorporate sourdough in your favorite yeast bread, counting the starter as part of your liquid. It will give it a different texture and flavor. Use the basic sourdough recipe as a model. Since even with yeast added, the rising time is slower than with breads made with commercial yeast, there is less danger of overproofing.

Sourdough starter also makes delicious pancakes and muffins.

Basic White Sourdough Bread

Remove the starter from the refrigerator several hours before using. The sponge will work better if all ingredients are at room temperature.

To make a smooth sponge, sprinkle the flour into the milk or water and beat hard with a wire whisk. Then add the starter, stirring with a wooden spoon.

SPONGE

In the evening, mix together in a large bowl:

2 cups unbleached white flour
1½ cups lukewarm water or milk
1 cup starter

Let rise overnight, covered with plastic wrap and a towel, in a warm, draft-free place.

DOUGH

In the morning stir and *return 1 cup of sponge to starter*. Add to remaining sponge and mix well:

2 TBS. *soft butter, margarine, or oil*
2 TBS. *light brown sugar*
1 TBS. *active dry yeast dissolved in*
¼ *cup warm water with*
½ *tsp. sugar*

2 *tsp. salt*
1 *tsp. baking soda (optional)*
3½ *to 4 cups unbleached white flour*

Add 1 cup of flour and beat into the sponge, using a wooden paddle. If you wish to use the soda, mix it thoroughly into this cup. Beat in vigorously enough of the remaining flour to make the dough roll away from the sides of the bowl. Turn onto a floured board and knead until the dough is smooth and elastic, about 10 minutes. Form into a ball, place in an oiled bowl, and turn to coat both sides. Cover with plastic wrap, add a towel for warmth, and allow to rise at room temperature until double in bulk, about 1½ hours. Punch down and knead again for 5 to 10 minutes. Let rest for 10 minutes, covered with plastic. Divide in half, form two loaves, cover again, and let rise in greased pans until the dough reaches the top of the pans. Bake at 375° for 10 minutes, reduce the heat to 350°, and bake until done, about 20 to 30 minutes more. If you like a very crusty loaf, use water in place of milk, brush the top of the loaves with water just before putting into the oven, and place a pan of hot water on the oven floor. If you prefer a round or long loaf, bake on a greased cookie sheet that has been liberally sprinkled with cornmeal. Remember that free-form loaves require a stiffer dough than when baked in pans.

This basic recipe makes a very soft loaf that will not slice easily until the next day.

Yield: 2 loaves 8 by 4 by 2¼ inches.

For a dark loaf, substitute 1 to 3 cups of whole wheat or rye flour for an equal amount of white, and use either dark brown sugar, molasses, or honey.

White Sourdough Bread

A solid, chewy bread of good flavor and texture. Makes excellent toast.

Remove the starter from the refrigerator several hours before using. All ingredients should be at room temperature.

SPONGE

In the evening mix together in a large bowl:

3 cups unbleached white flour	¾ cup lukewarm milk
1 cup lukewarm potato water	1 cup starter

Let rise overnight, covered with plastic wrap and a towel, in a warm, draft-free place.

DOUGH

In the morning stir sponge and *return 1 cup of sponge to starter.* Add to remaining sponge and mix well:

2 TBS. honey	2 tsp. salt
2 TBS. cooking oil	½ tsp. baking soda (optional)
1 TBS. active dry yeast dissolved in	¼ cup raw wheat germ
¼ cup warm water with ½ tsp. sugar	2 to 2¼ cups unbleached white flour

Mix salt, soda, and wheat germ thoroughly into 1 cup of flour and beat it into the sponge, using a wooden spoon or paddle.

Add enough of the remaining flour so that the dough leaves the sides of the bowl. Turn onto a well-floured board and knead for 10 minutes or until the dough is elastic and shows blisters at the surface. Place in an oiled bowl, turn to coat both sides, cover with plastic wrap and a towel, and let rise in a warm, draft-free place until double in bulk. Knead again for 10 minutes. Cover with plastic wrap and let rest while you clean up. Shape into a loaf, place in a greased bread pan, cover with greased plastic wrap and a towel, and let rise until the dough is an inch above the pan in the center. Bake at 375° for 10 minutes; reduce heat to 350° and bake for 30 to 40 minutes more, until the loaf sounds hollow when thumped on the bottom. Remove from pan and cool on a wire rack.

Yield: 1 loaf.

English Muffin Sourdough Bread

This bread should be eaten toasted. It is excellent.

Remove the starter from the refrigerator several hours before using. All ingredients should be at room temperature.

SPONGE

In the evening mix together in a large bowl:

2¼ cups unbleached white flour
1¼ cups warm milk
1 cup starter

Let rise overnight, covered with plastic wrap and a towel, in a warm draft-free place.

DOUGH

In the morning stir sponge and *return 1 cup of sponge to starter.*
Add to remaining sponge and mix well:

2 TBS. very soft butter or
    margarine
2½ tsp. light brown sugar
1 TBS. active dry yeast
    dissolved in
¼ cup warm water with
½ tsp. sugar

2 tsp. salt
2 cups white flour
½ tsp. baking soda
    (optional, for less
    sour bread)

Add 1 cup of flour and beat into the sponge, using a wooden paddle. If you wish to use the baking soda, mix it thoroughly into this cup. Beat in vigorously enough of the remaining flour to make the dough roll away from the sides of the bowl. It will be very sticky. *Do not knead.* Cover with plastic wrap and a towel and let rise in a warm, draft-free place until double in bulk. Stir down with 25 strokes. Fill greased pans half full, cover with greased plastic wrap and a towel, and let rise until the dough just reaches the top of the pan. If it rises too high the bread will slump in the middle during baking. If it should rise too high, beat it down and let it rise again. Bake at 375° for 30 to 35 minutes. Remove from pans and, when the bread has cooled, wrap in plastic and place in a plastic bag. The bread will be very soft the first day. Do not slice until the next day.

Yield: 1 large or 2 small loaves.

Sourdough English Muffins

Follow exactly the recipe given for English Muffin Sourdough Bread to the first rising of the dough. Allow to rise in a warm, draft-free place for 3 hours. The dough will more than double in bulk, which is necessary to achieve the proper texture for muffins.

Then stir down with 25 strokes. Flour your hands and make the dough into balls about 1½ inches in diameter. Place on a greased cookie sheet that has been generously dusted with cornmeal. Cover with wax paper and flatten. Let rise until light, ½ hour or more, and cook on a preheated greased skillet or griddle at medium heat until the bottom is nicely brown. Reduce heat one setting, turn muffins, and brown the other side. Cool on wire racks. Break apart with a fork, toast, and serve drenched in butter. Delicious!

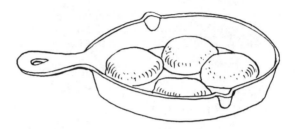

Yield: Approximately 16 muffins.

Whole Wheat Sourdough Bread

A robust loaf of good flavor, this makes a fine luncheon bread.

Remove the starter from the refrigerator several hours before using. All ingredients should be at room temperature.

SPONGE

In the evening, mix together in a large bowl:

2¼ cups unbleached white flour
1½ cups lukewarm milk
1 cup starter

Cover with plastic wrap and a towel and let rise overnight in a warm, draft-free place.

Dough

In the morning stir the sponge and *return 1 cup of sponge to starter*.

Add to the remaining sponge and mix well:

3 TBS. *honey*
3 TBS. *sesame oil*
½ cup *wheat germ*
2 tsp. *salt*
½ tsp. *crushed cumin seed*

1½ TBS. *active dry yeast*
   dissolved in
¼ cup *warm water with*
½ tsp. *sugar*
2 cups *whole wheat flour*
1 tsp. *baking soda*
   (optional)

Beat vigorously with a wooden spoon. Add additional white flour if necessary to make the dough roll away from the bowl, using as little as possible, or the bread will be dry. Turn onto a lightly floured board and knead for 10 minutes. Place in an oiled bowl, turn to coat both sides, cover with plastic wrap and a towel, and let rise in a warm, draft-free place until double in bulk. Knead again for 10 minutes. Divide in two, cover with plastic wrap, and let rest while you clean up. Then form into two loaves. Place in greased bread pans, cover with greased plastic wrap and a towel, and let rise until the dough is an inch above the pan in the center. Bake at 375° for 10 minutes; reduce heat to 325° and bake for about 40 minutes, or until the loaf sounds hollow when rapped on the bottom. Remove from the pans immediately, brush with butter, and cool on wire racks.

Yield: 1 large loaf or 2 small ones.

Bran and Wheat Germ Sourdough Bread

A sturdy bread with a different flavor.

All ingredients should be at room temperature.

SPONGE

In the evening mix together in a large bowl:

1¾ cups unbleached white flour
2 cups lukewarm milk
1 cup starter

DOUGH

In the morning stir sponge and *return 1 cup of sponge to starter.*
Add to the remaining sponge and mix well:

2 TBS. *very soft butter or margarine*	¼ tsp. *mace*
3 TBS. *honey*	1 TBS. *active dry yeast dissolved in*
1 *egg, beaten*	¼ cup *warm water with*
2 tsp. *salt*	½ tsp. *sugar*
1 cup *flaky bran flour*	2 to 2½ cups *white flour*
½ cup *raw wheat germ*	½ tsp. *baking soda (optional)*

Beat thoroughly with a wooden spoon or paddle and add just enough flour to make the dough roll away from the bowl. Turn onto a floured board and knead until the dough is smooth and elastic, about 10 minutes. Form into a ball, place in an oiled bowl, and turn to coat both sides. Cover with plastic wrap, add a towel for warmth, and allow to rise in a warm, draft-free place until double in bulk, about 1½ hours. Punch down and knead again for 10 minutes. Let rest for 10 minutes, covering with plastic wrap. Divide in half, shape into two loaves, and place in greased pans. Cover with greased plastic wrap and let rise again until the dough is just above the sides of the pans. Bake in 375° oven for 10 minutes; reduce heat to 350° and bake for 30 to 40 minutes more, or until the bread sounds hollow when tapped. Remove from pans and cool on wire racks.

Yield: 2 average loaves.

Rye Sourdough Bread

A very good, light, and tangy bread.

Remove the starter from the refrigerator several hours before using. All ingredients should be at room temperature.

SPONGE

In the evening mix together in a large bowl:

2 ¼ cups unbleached white flour
1 ¼ cups lukewarm milk
1 cup starter

Cover with plastic wrap and a towel and let rise overnight in a warm, draft-free place.

DOUGH

In the morning stir sponge and *return 1 cup of sponge to starter.* Add to the remaining sponge and mix well:

2 TBS. very soft butter or margarine	1 TBS. active dry yeast dissolved in
2 TBS. dark brown sugar	¼ cup warm water with
2 TBS. cornmeal	½ tsp. sugar

Sift together and add:

1 cup rye flour	½ tsp. baking soda (optional, for a less tangy bread)
1 tsp. salt	

Beat vigorously with a wooden spoon or paddle.
Add if needed:

¼ to ½ cup white flour

Use only enough white flour to make the dough roll away from the sides of the bowl. It will be very sticky, so start kneading in the bowl. When it has become less sticky, turn onto a floured board and knead for 10 minutes, until the dough is elastic and satiny and shows bubbles at the surface. Place in an oiled bowl, turn to coat both sides, cover with plastic wrap and a towel, and let rise in a warm, draft-free place until double in bulk, about 1¼ hours. Knead again for 10 minutes. Divide into two pieces, cover with the plastic, and let rest for 10 minutes. Shape into two balls. Place on a greased cookie sheet that has been liberally sprinkled with cornmeal, cover with greased plastic wrap and a towel, and let rise again until nearly double in bulk. Bake at 375° for 10 minutes; reduce heat to 325° and bake for 20 to 30 minutes. The bread is done when it sounds hollow when rapped on the bottom. For a shiny crust, 5 minutes before the bread is done glaze with white of an egg beaten into 1 tablespoon of water. Remove from the cookie sheet and cool on a wire rack.

Yield: 2 loaves.

VARIATION

Whole wheat may be substituted for the rye flour. For oatmeal bread substitute 1½ cups of oatmeal for the rye flour, increase the white flour to nearly a cup, and use 3 tablespoons of molasses instead of the brown sugar. The resulting loaves will be blander, heavier, and sweeter than the rye bread, but good.

Rye Buttermilk Sourdough Bread

A delicately textured bread with the authentic sourdough tang.

Have all ingredients at room temperature.

SPONGE

In the evening mix together in a large bowl:

2 cups unbleached white flour
1½ cups lukewarm buttermilk
1 cup starter

Cover with plastic wrap and a towel and let rise overnight in a warm, draft-free place.

Dough

In the morning stir sponge and *return 1 cup of sponge to starter*.

Add to the remaining sponge and beat vigorously with a wooden spoon or paddle:

3 TBS. dark brown sugar
2 TBS. very soft butter or
  margarine
2 tsp. salt

1 TBS. active dry yeast
  dissolved in
¼ cup warm water with
½ tsp. sugar
2 cups rye flour
½ tsp. baking soda (optional)

If necessary, add enough white flour to make the dough roll away from the bowl. Turn onto a lightly floured board and knead for 10 minutes or until the dough is satiny and elastic and air bubbles show at the surface. Place in an oiled bowl, turning to coat both sides. Cover with plastic wrap and a towel and let rise in a warm, draft-free place until double in bulk, about 1 to 1¼ hours. Knead again for 10 minutes, cover with plastic, and let rest while you clean up. Shape into one large loaf or two small ones. Place in greased pans, cover with greased plastic wrap and a towel, and let rise until the dough has risen just above the sides of the pan, about ¾ hour. Bake at 375° for 10 minutes; reduce heat to 350° and bake 30 minutes for small loaves and longer for a large one. Remove from pans immediately and cool on wire racks. If you would like a shiny crust, 5 minutes before you remove the bread from the oven, brush with a glaze made of the white of an egg beaten into 1 tablespoon of water, and return loaf to the oven.

Yield: 1 large loaf or 2 small ones.

Substitute whole wheat flour for the rye. This will not be as tangy, but is nevertheless very good.

Caraway Rye Sourdough Bread

The different ingredients give this rye bread a very different flavor from the other two.

The ingredients should be at room temperature.

SPONGE

In the evening mix together in a large bowl:

2 cups unbleached white flour
1¼ cups lukewarm water
1 cup starter

Cover with plastic wrap and a towel and let rise overnight in a warm, draft-free place.

DOUGH

In the morning stir sponge and *return 1 cup of sponge to starter.* Add to the remaining sponge and mix well:

1½ cups warm water
¼ cup dark brown sugar
½ to 1 tsp. caraway or
  cumin seeds, crushed
1 TBS. instant coffee
2 tsp. salt

3 TBS. sesame oil
1 TBS. active dry yeast
  dissolved in
¼ cup warm water with
1 tsp. sugar

148

Mix well and add:

4½ cups rye flour

Beat vigorously with wooden spoon or paddle and add:

1 to 1½ cups white flour
½ tsp. baking soda (optional)

or just enough to make the dough roll away from the bowl. Turn onto a floured board and knead for 10 minutes or until the dough is satiny and elastic and air bubbles appear at the surface. Place in an oiled bowl, turn to coat both sides, cover with plastic wrap and a towel, and let rise in a warm, draft-free place until double in bulk. Knead again for 10 minutes. Divide into two balls, cover with the plastic, and let rest while you clean up. Shape into two loaves. Place in greased bread pans, cover with greased plastic wrap and the towel, and let rise until the dough is an inch above the pan in the center. Or bake them in greased casseroles or pie pans for attractive round loaves. This dough is too sticky for free-form loaves. Bake at 375° for 10 minutes; reduce heat to 325° and bake for 35 to 45 minutes longer, or until the loaf sounds hollow when tapped on the bottom. Turn out of pans immediately and cool on wire racks.

VARIATION

Instead of the 4½ cups of rye flour, use 2½ cups of rye flour and 2 cups of whole wheat, well mixed together.

Yield: 2 loaves.

Cornmeal Sourdough Bread

A tangy sourdough version of cornmeal batter bread.

All ingredients should be at room temperature.

SPONGE

In the evening mix together in a large bowl:

2 cups unbleached white flour
1½ cups lukewarm buttermilk
1 cup starter

Cover with plastic wrap and a towel and let rise overnight in a warm, draft-free place.

DOUGH

In the morning stir the sponge and *return 1 cup of sponge to starter*.

Add to the remaining sponge and mix well:

2 TBS. very soft butter or
  margarine
2 TBS. light brown sugar
2 tsp. salt
2 eggs

1 TBS. active dry yeast
  dissolved in
¼ cup warm water with
½ tsp. sugar

Mix well and add:

1½ cups yellow cornmeal

Beat vigorously with wooden spoon or paddle and add:

2¼ to 2½ cups unbleached white flour
½ tsp. baking soda (optional)

or just enough to make the dough roll away from the bowl. Turn onto a floured board and knead for 10 minutes, or until the dough is satiny and elastic and has a dimpled appearance. Place in an oiled bowl, turn to coat both sides, cover with plastic wrap and a towel, and let rise in a warm, draft-free place until double in bulk, about 1¼ hours. Knead again for 10 minutes. Divide into two balls, cover with plastic wrap, and let rest while you clean up. Shape into two loaves. Place in greased bread pans, cover with greased plastic wrap, and let rise until

150

the dough is an inch above the pans in the center. Or bake them in greased casseroles or pie pans for attractive round loaves. Bake at 375° for 10 minutes; reduce heat to 350° and bake for 30 minutes more, or until the loaf sounds hollow when tapped on the bottom. Turn out of pans immediately and cool on wire racks.

Yield: 2 average loaves.

Pumpkin Sourdough Bread

A good company bread.

All ingredients should be at room temperature.

SPONGE

In the evening mix together in a large bowl:

2 cups unbleached white flour
1½ cups lukewarm milk
1 cup starter

Cover with plastic wrap and a towel and let rise in a warm, draft-free place overnight.

DOUGH

In the morning stir the sponge and *return 1 cup of sponge to starter.*
Add to the remaining sponge:

1½ cups puréed pumpkin,
   fresh or canned
3 TBS. very soft butter or
   margarine
¾ cup dark brown sugar,
   tightly packed

1 egg
1 TBS. active dry yeast
   dissolved in
¼ cup warm water with
½ tsp. sugar
2 tsp. salt

Mix well and add, sifted together:

½ tsp. cinnamon   1½ cups graham flour
¾ tsp. crushed cardamom   ½ tsp. baking soda
¼ tsp. ginger   (optional)

Beat vigorously with a wooden spoon and add:

4½ to 5 cups unbleached white flour

or enough to make the dough roll away from the bowl. Turn onto a floured board and knead for 10 minutes or until the dough is satiny and elastic and has a dimpled appearance. Place in an oiled bowl, turn to coat both sides, cover with plastic wrap and a towel, and let rise in a warm, draft-free place until double in bulk, about 1½ hours. Knead again for 10 minutes. Divide into two balls, cover with plastic wrap, and let rest while you clean up. Shape into two loaves, place in greased bread pans, cover with greased plastic wrap, and let rise until the dough is an inch above the pans in the center. Bake at 375° for 10 minutes; reduce heat to 350° and bake 35 to 40 minutes longer, or until the loaf sounds hollow when tapped on the bottom. Turn out of pans immediately and cool on wire racks.

Yield: 2 average loaves.

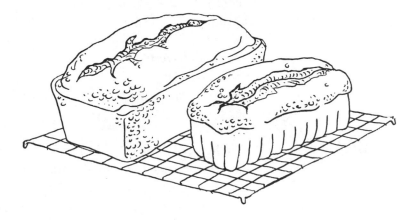

10 Quick Breads

Quick breads are what their name implies—quick to make—and they are most useful breads for this reason. They rely on baking powder or baking soda for leavening, instead of yeast, eliminating the long rising periods. All the recipes in this book call for double-acting baking powder. If you use single-acting, adjust the amount according to directions on the can. With either type, do not let the batter rise before baking, unless the recipe specifically says so. It should go into the oven at once.

Usually quick breads are sweet, but we have produced some excellent ones that are not sweet and therefore are good with soups and luncheon dishes.

Eat these breads quickly after baking, for with a few exceptions, they dry out faster than yeast breads, and also tend to dry out when frozen. However, quick breads may be refreshed by placing a loaf in a damp paper bag and reheating for 10 minutes in a 350° oven.

Quick breads must be handled more delicately than yeast breads and assembled rapidly and deftly, with a light hand.

Basic Quick Bread

All ingredients must be at room temperature.

1½ cups lukewarm liquid
3 cups flour
1 tsp. salt
1 TBS. double-acting
  baking powder
2 TBS. to 1 cup sugar

2 to 4 TBS. butter or margarine
  (optional—makes a richer
  bread that keeps better)
1 to 2 eggs (optional—makes
  a finer textured, lighter
  and richer bread)

MIXING METHODS

A simple quick bread should *never* be beaten, but stirred together gently. Beating makes tough, dry bread of coarse texture, full of holes and tunnels, and of low volume. Sift the dry ingredients together in a large bowl, and combine the liquids in another. Make a well in the dry ingredients and pour in the liquids all at once. Mix very lightly until the dry mixture is just moistened. The batter will be lumpy.

A quick bread that resembles a cake in having much richer ingredients should be mixed like one, creaming butter and sugar, adding the eggs. Add alternately the dry ingredients that have been sifted together, and the milk.

For a very delicate bread, beat yolks and white of eggs separately, beating the whites until they are dry. Add the yolks to the batter, or in a rich batter, to the butter and sugar, gently folding in the whites at the end.

Fill pans three-quarters full, for quick breads will not rise as high as yeast breads. Just before putting pans in the oven, cut through the batter lengthwise with a wet knife, to a depth of ½ inch. These breads break during baking and this will cause them to break along the center line, making a better appearing loaf.

Quick breads need less heat, 300° to 325° as a rule, and a longer baking period, about 1 to 1½ hours. Too much heat will cause holes in the bread. Let the loaf cool for 5 to 10 minutes after removing from the oven before turning out on a wire rack to cool. If you are using a fancy mold or fluted pan, let stand for about 10 to 15 minutes for easier removal.

Pastry flour may be used in quick breads (though never in yeast breads). You will need 2 tablespoons more flour per cup than when using bread flour.

For spice breads, add:

1 teaspoon cinnamon
½ teaspoon nutmeg
½ cup nuts or raisins, or both

If using heavy, dark flours, or fruits and nuts, increase baking powder to 1½ tsp. per cup of flour.

Fruits give a good flavor to bread. Use 1 cup of stewed or strained fruits. If using strained fruits, reduce liquid to ¾ cup. If you are using sour milk, buttermilk, or sour cream, add ½ tsp. baking soda to each cup of liquid. This will make a lighter bread.

Yield: 1 loaf 8¼ by 4¼ by 2½ inches.

Maltex Quick Bread

Quick, easy, and marvelous!

1 cup Maltex cereal
2 cups unbleached
  white flour
¼ cup raw wheat germ
1 TBS. double-acting
  baking powder

1 tsp. salt
½ tsp. baking soda
2 TBS. light brown sugar
1¾ cups lukewarm
  buttermilk
2 TBS. cooking oil

Sift together the dry ingredients into a large bowl. In another bowl mix together the buttermilk and oil. Make a well in the dry ingredients and pour in the liquid mixture all at once. Mix together gently and quickly until the dry ingredients are just moistened. The batter will be lumpy. Pour into a greased loaf pan, cover with plastic wrap, and allow to rise for 15 minutes. Bake at 325° for 50 to 60 minutes. The bread is done when it shrinks from the sides of the pan and when a toothpick inserted into the center comes out clean. Let cool in the pan for 5 minutes and turn out onto a wire rack to cool.

Yield: 1 loaf.

For a sweet tea loaf, use ½ cup of light brown sugar.

Kasha Bread

A chewy bread with a crisp crust and a whole grain flavor, this is great with soups and salads.

2 cups unbleached white flour
½ cup buckwheat flour
¼ tsp. crushed cumin seed
2 tsp. salt
4 tsp. double-acting
   baking powder

2 TBS. dark brown sugar
1 egg, separated
2 cups lukewarm milk
1½ TBS. cooking oil
1 cup cooked Kasha
   (buckwheat groats)

In a large bowl sift together the flour, cumin, salt, baking powder, and sugar. In another bowl mix together the slightly beaten egg yolk, milk, oil, and the Kasha (cooked according to directions on package). Make a well in the dry ingredients and add the milk mixture all at once, stirring gently and rapidly until just moistened. The batter will be lumpy. Lightly fold in the egg white, which has been beaten until dry. Spoon batter into a greased loaf pan. Slash with a wet knife lengthwise through the top of the loaf, about ½ inch deep. Cover with plastic wrap and let rise for 15 minutes. Bake at 350° for about 1 hour. The bread is done when it shrinks away from the sides of the pan and when a toothpick inserted in the center comes out clean. Cool in pan for 5 minutes, then turn out onto a wire rack.

Yield: 1 large loaf or 2 small ones.

Whole Wheat Bread

Fine for luncheons and sandwiches, and toasted for breakfast. It has a delightful flavor and a crunchy crust.

1 cup whole wheat flour	¼ cup dark brown sugar
2 cups unbleached white flour	½ tsp. (scant) crushed cumin seed
4 tsp. double-acting baking powder	¼ cup raw wheat germ
2 tsp. salt	1½ TBS. sesame oil
	2 cups lukewarm milk

Sift together all the dry ingredients. In another bowl mix the oil and milk together. Make a well in the dry ingredients and pour in the milk mixture all at once. Mix together gently and quickly until the dry ingredients are just moistened. The batter will be lumpy. Pour into a greased loaf pan, slash lengthwise with a sharp, wet knife, and bake at 325° for approximately 1¼ hours. The bread is done when it shrinks from the sides of the pan and when a toothpick inserted in the center comes out clean. Let cool in the pan for 5 minutes and turn out onto a wire rack.

Yield: 1 loaf.

VARIATION

For a sweeter tea bread, use ½ cup sugar. Make a topping of ⅓ cup of Quaker 100% Natural Cereal which has had the lumps rolled out, and 2 tablespoons of melted butter. Sprinkle this mixture over the loaf just before putting in the oven, and press gently into the batter.

Grandmother Loren's Brown Bread

This is an outstanding bread and, unlike most quick breads, it keeps well for many days. It also freezes well. Our thanks to Mary J. Strudwick for allowing us to use her grandmother's recipe.

2 cups graham flour	1½ tsp. baking soda
1 cup unbleached white flour	4 tsp. double-acting baking powder
1 cup light brown sugar	2 cups lukewarm sour milk or buttermilk
1 tsp. salt	

Sift all the dry ingredients together. Add the milk, stirring it in gently until the flour mixture is just moistened. The dough will be soft. Spoon into a greased loaf pan, and slash lengthwise with a sharp knife. Bake at 300° for 1 to 1¼ hours. It is done when a toothpick inserted in the center comes out clean. Let cool in pan for 5 minutes and turn out onto a wire rack.

Yield: 1 large loaf.

VARIATION

Substitute whole wheat flour for the graham, using dark brown sugar and an extra ⅓ cup of milk. This makes a very good, rather sweet bread. Sugar may be cut in half if desired.

Or substitute 1 cup of rye flour for 1 cup of graham, keeping other ingredients the same.

Irish Soda Bread

This authentic Irish recipe is best eaten when warm and crusty. It is not a good keeper.

⅓ cup butter
4 cups unbleached
   white flour
1 TBS. double-acting
   baking powder
1 tsp. baking soda

1 tsp. salt
¼ cup light brown sugar
1 cup raisins
1 egg
1½ cups lukewarm butter-
   milk, approximately

If the raisins are hard and dry, refresh them by placing in a saucepan and covering with cold water. Bring to a boil, remove from heat, and let stand for 5 minutes. Drain well, spread on a paper, and pat dry.

Cut the butter into the flour as you would for pastry. Mix the baking powder, baking soda, salt, and sugar together thoroughly and add the raisins. Add to the flour mixture, combining thoroughly.

158

Beat the egg slightly and add to 1 cup of buttermilk. Pour over the dry ingredients, stirring in enough of the remaining milk to form a dough. Turn onto a floured board and knead for a couple of minutes. Form a flattened ball and place in a greased iron frying pan. With a sharp knife, cut a deep cross on top, right to the edges. Bake in a 375° oven for 35 to 45 minutes, or until a toothpick inserted in the center comes out clean. Remove from oven and immediately turn out of pan onto a wire rack to cool.

Yield: 1 large loaf.

Whole Wheat Irish Soda Bread

A most satisfying whole wheat version of the preceding Irish Soda Bread and, like it, best eaten when warm.

2 cups unbleached white flour	2 tsp. double-acting baking powder
⅓ cup butter	3 TBS. light brown sugar
2 cups whole wheat flour	1 cup dark raisins
1 tsp. salt	1 egg, beaten
1 heaping tsp. baking soda	1½ cups lukewarm buttermilk

Place the white flour in a large bowl and cut the butter into it, as you would for pastry. In another bowl, mix together thoroughly the whole wheat flour, salt, baking soda, baking powder, and brown sugar, then stir in the raisins. Add to the white flour mixture, mixing well. Add the beaten egg to the buttermilk and stir into the dry ingredients. Turn onto a floured board and knead a few minutes, until smooth. Form a flattened ball and place in a greased iron skillet. With a sharp knife, cut a deep cross on top, right to the edges. Bake at 375° for 35 to 45 minutes, until a toothpick inserted in the center comes out clean. Remove from pan and cool on a wire rack.

Yield: 1 large loaf.

Maple Bread

A delicious sweet bread with a real maple flavor.

½ cup sweet butter
2 eggs, beaten separately
½ cup lukewarm milk
¾ cup maple syrup
1 lemon rind, grated

2 cups unbleached
    white flour
1 TBS. double-acting
    baking powder
1 tsp. salt

Cream the butter until soft and light. Beat the egg yolks and add to the butter. Add the milk, syrup, and rind and mix well. Sift together the flour, baking powder, and salt into a medium sized bowl. Pour the liquid mixture over it all at once, and mix gently until the dry ingredients are just moistened. Fold in the stiffly beaten egg whites and pour the batter into a greased loaf pan. Slash lengthwise with a sharp, wet knife. Bake at 375° for 10 minutes; reduce heat to 350° and bake for about 30 to 35 minutes, or until a toothpick inserted into the center of the loaf comes out clean. Let cool for 5 minutes before turning onto a wire rack to cool.

Yield: 1 average loaf.

Orange Marmalade Bread

A delicious tea bread, easily prepared.

4 TBS. butter
½ cup sugar
2 eggs, separated
Rind and juice of
    1 large orange
6 TBS. thick, bitter
    orange marmalade

Lukewarm milk
2½ cups unbleached
    white flour
1 tsp. salt
4 tsp. double-acting
    baking powder

Cream the butter and sugar together until light. Beat yolks of eggs well and add to the butter mixture. Reserve 1 teaspoon of orange

160

rind and 3 tablespoons of juice. Add the rest of the rind to the mixture. Place the orange marmalade in a 2-cup measure, add the remaining orange juice and enough milk to make 1½ cups, stirring well. Sift the flour, salt, and baking powder together and add alternately with the milk mixture, to the butter mixture. Gently fold in the white of eggs beaten until they are dry. Pour the batter into a greased loaf pan. With a knife cut a slash lengthwise through the center a half inch deep. Bake at 325° for about 1 hour. The bread is done when it shrinks from the sides of the pan and when a toothpick inserted in the center comes out clean. Glaze immediately upon taking from the oven with the reserved orange rind and juice mixed into ½ cup of sifted confectioners' sugar. Let stand for 5 minutes before turning out onto a wire rack to cool.

Yield: 1 average loaf.

St. John's Bread (Carob)

A moist tea bread with a chocolate flavor, this keeps very well.

¾ cup sugar
½ cup butter or margarine
1 tsp. salt
½ cup lukewarm milk
2 eggs, separated
1 ripe banana

2 cups unbleached
  white flour
½ cup carob powder,
  toasted
1 TBS. double-acting
  baking powder

Cream together the sugar and butter until light. Add the salt, milk, and well-beaten egg yolks. Crush the banana with a silver fork and add to the mixture. Sift together the flour, carob powder, and baking powder into a bowl. Add the liquid mixture all at once, stirring lightly until the dry ingredients are just moistened. Beat the egg whites until they are dry and gently fold into the batter. Place the mixture into a greased bread pan, slash lengthwise with a sharp and wet knife, and bake in a preheated 350° oven for about 1 hour. The bread is done when it shrinks away from the sides of the pan and when a toothpick inserted into the center of the loaf comes out clean. Let the bread cool in the pan for 5 minutes before turning out onto a wire rack.

Yield: 1 loaf.

Nut Bread

Another nut bread? The graham flour in this recipe found among family papers gives the bread a unique flavor.

2 cups graham flour	1 TBS. double-acting
2 cups unbleached	baking powder
white flour	1 cup chopped English
1 tsp. salt	walnuts
1 cup sugar	2 eggs
	1½ cups lukewarm milk

Sift into a bowl all the dry ingredients. Add the walnuts. In another bowl mix together the eggs and milk. Make a well in the dry ingredients and pour in the liquid mixture all at once. Mix together gently and quickly until the dry ingredients are just moistened. The batter will be lumpy. Pour into two small greased pans, 7½ by 4 by 2 inches. Let rise for 20 minutes and bake in a 325° oven for 1 to 1¼ hours. The bread is done when it shrinks from the sides of the pan and when a toothpick inserted in the center comes out clean. Let cool in the pan for 5 minutes and turn onto a wire rack to cool.

Yield: 2 small loaves.

Boston Brown Bread

Authentic Boston Brown Bread is steamed on top of the stove for 3 hours. This oven-steamed version is quicker, cooking for 1½ hours, and is very good.

2 cups lukewarm buttermilk	1 cup cornmeal
1 cup molasses	1 cup rye flour
1 tsp. baking soda	2 cups unbleached
1 tsp. double-acting	white flour
baking powder	½ tsp. salt
	¾ cup dark raisins

Heat buttermilk and molasses until lukewarm. Mix all dry ingredients together thoroughly. Gradually add the buttermilk mixture to the dry ingredients, beating after each addition. Fold in the raisins. Pour the batter into two very well-greased one-pound coffee cans. Cover with greased aluminum foil and crimp, but do not tie on. Place the cans in a kettle of boiling water deep enough to cover the lower half of the cans, adding boiling water as needed to maintain that level. Bake on the lower rack of a 375° oven for about 1½ hours or until a wooden skewer inserted into the center (first removing the foil cap) comes out clean. Remove the cans from the oven, remove foil cap, and allow them to stand on a wire rack for 10 minutes before removing the bread. Cool on the rack.

Yield: 2 loaves.

Carrot Bread

A rich, moist, cakelike bread, lovely at tea time. Don't be put off by the carrots; even the children love it.

4 TBS. butter or margarine	½ tsp. allspice
½ cup dark brown sugar	½ tsp. salt
1 egg	2 cups unbleached
1 jar junior baby food	white flour
carrots or 1 cup grated	2 tsp. double-acting
fresh carrots	baking powder
	½ cup lukewarm milk
	½ cup light golden raisins

Cream together butter and brown sugar, add lightly beaten egg and the carrots. Sift the dry ingredients and fold into the butter mixture, alternating dry ingredients with milk. Fold in raisins which have been plumped in boiling water and dried on paper towels. Spoon into two small loaf pans measuring about 6 by 3¾ by 2 inches, or one larger, narrow pan. Cut lengthwise down the center of the batter with a knife. Bake at 375° for 15 minutes, reduce heat to 350°, and bake for about 40 minutes more or until the bread pulls away from the sides of the pans and a toothpick inserted into the center comes out clean. Let stand 5 minutes and turn onto a wire rack. Allow to cool before slicing.

Yield: 2 small or 1 average loaf.

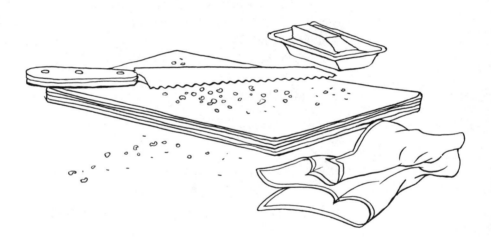

Index

168